Florence Travel

Updated and Complete Travel Manual

Carl Laws

Copyright Notice © 2025 by Carl Laws.

All rights reserved.

This publication is protected under copyright law. No part of this work may be copied, reproduced, distributed, or transmitted in any form or by any means—electronic, mechanical, photocopying, recording, or otherwise—without the prior written permission of the author or publisher, except for brief quotations used in reviews, critiques, or other legally permitted uses under copyright law. Unauthorized use or duplication is strictly prohibited.

Table of Contents

Introduction 7

    How to Use This Travel Guide 8

Welcome to Florence 11

    What Makes Florence Special? 12

    Quick Facts at a Glance 13

    A Snapshot of Its History and Culture 14

Chapter 1 17

Planning Your Visit 17

    Choosing the Best Time to Go 17

    Trip Budgeting Tips and Tricks 19

    Visa, Entry Requirements, and Documentation 22

    Staying Healthy and Safe: Travel Insurance, Vaccines,
    and Local Health Tips 24

Chapter 2 28

Getting to Florence 28

    Transportation Options: Air, Land, and Sea 28

    Major Airports and Arrival Hubs 33

    Insider Tips for Flights, Trains, and Overland Routes .. 35

    Overland Routes: Buses & Road Trips 38

Chapter 3 41

Getting Around Florence 41

    Public Transport: Everything You Need to Know 41

    Renting Cars, Scooters, and Other Vehicles 46

Walking and Cycling Routes for Explorers 49

Must-Have Apps for Navigation and Travel 54

Handy Local Maps and Orientation 57

Chapter 4 60

Where to Stay 60

Accommodation Choices: From Luxury Resorts to Cozy
Budget Stays 60

Unique and Memorable Stays (Eco-Lodges, Treehouses,
and More) 62

Top Neighborhoods and Areas to Stay 64

Best Picks for Families, Groups, and Solo Travelers ... 66

Chapter 5 69

Top Attractions and Landmarks 69

Iconic Sites You Need to See 69

Cultural and Historical Highlights 73

Hidden Gems for Off-the-Beaten-Path Adventures 75

Best Spots for Photography and Scenic Views 78

Fun and Memorable Family-Friendly Attractions 82

Chapter 6 87

Things to Do: Activities and Experiences 87

Outdoor Adventures (Hiking, Diving, Ziplining, and
More) 87

Neighborhood Strolls and Guided Tours 90

Local Experiences: Cooking, Crafting, and Cultural Immersion 93

Seasonal Highlights: Festivals, Events, and Activities . 96

Nature and Wildlife Adventures 99

Chapter 7 105

Food and Drink Scene.. 105

Can't-Miss Local Dishes and Drinks........................... 105

Best Restaurants, Cafes, and Bars for Every Budget.. 108

Cooking Classes and Foodie Experiences 114

Chapter 8 118

Cultural Insights.. 118

Local Customs, Traditions, and Etiquette................... 118

Phrases to Know in the Local Language..................... 121

Festivals, Celebrations, and Holidays to Plan Around 123

Exploring Local Art, Music, and Performances 126

Chapter 9 130

Shopping and Souvenirs 130

Best Shopping Spots: Malls, Markets, and Boutiques 130

Authentic Local Crafts and One-of-a-Kind Finds 133

Smart Bargaining Tips and Shopping Etiquette.......... 137

Chapter 10 142

Travel with a Conscience: Sustainable Tourism............ 142

Eco-Friendly Activities and Green Travel Options 142

Supporting Local Businesses and Communities......... 144

How to Minimize Your Carbon Footprint While Traveling
.... 146

Tips for Responsible Tourism.................................... 147

Chapter 11 149

Practical Information and Travel Essentials 149

Currency, and Money-Saving Tips............................. 149

Emergency Numbers, Safety Advice, and Local Laws
.... 151

Internet Access, and Charging Devices 152

Packing Guide Based on Florence's Climate.............. 154

Chapter 12 157

Itineraries and Day Trips 157

Perfect 3-Day, 5-Day, and Week-Long Plans............. 157

5-Day Florence Itinerary.. 159

Week-Long Florence Itinerary................................... 161

Seasonal Travel Plans with Local Insights 164

Chapter 13 166

Insider Tips and Tricks 166

Avoiding Tourist Traps.. 166

How to Blend In Like a Local.................................... 168

Saving Money Without Sacrificing Experience 169

Conclusion 172

Introduction

Florence is a city that transcends time, a place where art, history, and culture come together to create an unforgettable experience. As the birthplace of the Renaissance, Florence is not just a city—it's an open-air museum, brimming with world-renowned masterpieces, stunning architecture, and captivating history at every corner. From the awe-inspiring **Duomo** to the picturesque **Ponte Vecchio**, Florence offers endless moments of discovery.

Whether you're a first-time visitor or a returning traveler, this guide is designed to help you navigate the best of Florence, uncover hidden gems, and immerse yourself in the city's vibrant culture. From iconic landmarks like the **Uffizi Gallery** and **Accademia Museum** to charming neighborhoods like **Oltrarno**, this guide will take you through Florence's must-see sights and off-the-beaten-path locations.

But Florence isn't just about sightseeing—it's also about experiencing the city like a local. This guide will show you how to blend in, savor the city's delicious food, and make the most of your time while avoiding the common tourist pitfalls. Whether you're interested in art, history, food, or shopping, Florence offers something for everyone.

So, pack your bags and get ready to explore Florence. This guide will ensure that you don't just visit the city, but experience it to the fullest. Let's dive into everything this beautiful, timeless city has to offer!

How to Use This Travel Guide

This guide is structured to help you make the most of your time in Florence, regardless of whether you have a few days or a week to explore. Here's how to navigate and get the most out of the sections:

- **Itineraries**: If you're short on time, start with the **perfect 3-day, 5-day, or week-long itineraries**. These are designed to guide you through the highlights of Florence, with suggestions for each day, balancing must-see landmarks and local experiences.

- **Day Trips and Excursions**: If you want to venture beyond the city, check out the **suggested day trips** to nearby towns like **Pisa**, **Siena**, or the **Chianti wine region**. Florence is perfectly positioned for day excursions, and this guide provides detailed suggestions to help you explore the Tuscan countryside.

- **Top Attractions and Hidden Gems**: You'll find sections on the **must-see attractions** as well as **hidden gems** that are often overlooked by tourists. From world-famous art collections to quaint neighborhoods, this guide will help you discover both the iconic and the lesser-known sides of Florence.

- **Local Insights**: Look for **local insights** throughout the guide, where I share tips on how to enjoy Florence like a local. This includes advice on how to blend in, where to eat, what to do, and how to navigate the city's unique culture.

- **Practical Information**: In the **Practical Information** section, you'll find essential tips on money, safety, transportation, and much more, so you're fully prepared for your trip.

- **Sustainable Tourism**: Lastly, this guide includes advice on **sustainable tourism**, offering eco-friendly activities, suggestions for minimizing your carbon footprint, and ways to support local businesses and communities.

Each section of this guide is designed to be flexible—use it to craft your own perfect trip, whether you're looking to immerse yourself in art, indulge in fine dining, or simply take in the beauty of Florence at your own pace.

With this guide in hand, you'll be well-equipped to experience Florence as it's meant to be experienced—rich in culture, history, and timeless beauty. Enjoy your journey through this magnificent city!

Welcome to Florence

Imagine strolling through cobblestone streets bathed in golden sunlight, the scent of freshly baked focaccia wafting through the air, and the distant hum of a street musician's violin echoing off centuries-old stone walls. This is Florence—a city where art, history, and la dolce vita intertwine in perfect harmony. Known as the cradle of the Renaissance, Florence is a living museum, a culinary paradise, and a romantic haven all rolled into one.

From the iconic dome of the Florence Cathedral to the serene Arno River that cuts through the city, every corner of Florence tells a story. Whether you're marveling at Michelangelo's *David*, sipping Chianti in a rustic enoteca, or simply people-watching in Piazza della Signoria, Florence has a way of captivating your heart and soul.

What Makes Florence Special?

Florence is more than just a destination—it's an experience. Here's what sets it apart:

1. **Art and History Come Alive**: Florence is the birthplace of the Renaissance, and its streets are lined with masterpieces by legends like Botticelli, Leonardo da Vinci, and Michelangelo. The Uffizi Gallery and Accademia Gallery are treasure troves of artistic brilliance.

2. **Architectural Marvels**: The city's skyline is dominated by the terracotta dome of the Florence Cathedral (Duomo), a feat of engineering that still leaves visitors in awe. The Ponte Vecchio, a medieval stone bridge lined with jewelry shops, is another iconic symbol of the city.

3. **Culinary Delights**: Florence is a food lover's dream. From hearty ribollita soup to melt-in-your-mouth bistecca alla Fiorentina (Florentine steak), the city's cuisine is as rich as its history. Don't forget to indulge in gelato from one of the city's artisanal shops!

4. **Charming Neighborhoods**: Each district has its own personality. The Oltrarno, on the south side of the Arno, is a bohemian haven filled with artisan workshops and cozy cafes. Meanwhile, the historic center buzzes with energy and grandeur.

5. **Timeless Romance**: Florence is the city of love. Whether it's watching the sunset from Piazzale Michelangelo or sharing a bottle of wine by the river, the city exudes romance at every turn.

6. **Gateway to Tuscany**: Florence is perfectly positioned for exploring the rolling hills, vineyards, and medieval villages of Tuscany. Day trips to Siena, Pisa, and the Chianti wine region are a must.

Florence is a city that invites you to slow down, savor the moment, and immerse yourself in its beauty. Whether you're a history buff, a foodie, or a hopeless romantic, Florence promises an unforgettable journey. Let's dive into the heart of this enchanting city and discover all it has to offer! 🌟

Quick Facts at a Glance

📍 **Location**: Florence is the capital of Italy's Tuscany region, nestled in the heart of central Italy.

🕒 **Best Time to Visit**: Spring (April–June) and Fall

(September–October) for mild weather and fewer crowds. Summer is busy but vibrant, while winter offers a quieter, more intimate experience.

🌐 **Population**: Approximately 380,000 residents.

💶 **Currency**: Euro (€).

🗣 **Language**: Italian, though English is widely spoken in tourist areas.

🚶 **Walkability**: Florence is compact and best explored on foot. Most major attractions are within walking distance of each other.

🏆 **Famous For**: Renaissance art, historic architecture, Tuscan cuisine, and world-class wine.

A Snapshot of Its History and Culture

Florence's story begins over 2,000 years ago, when it was founded as a Roman settlement in 59 BCE. However, it was during the Middle Ages and the Renaissance that Florence truly flourished, becoming a powerhouse of art, culture, and commerce.

1. **The Birthplace of the Renaissance**: In the 14th to 17th centuries, Florence was the epicenter of the Renaissance, a cultural movement that reshaped Europe. Wealthy families like the Medici patronized

artists, architects, and thinkers, leading to an explosion of creativity. This era gave us masterpieces like Botticelli's *The Birth of Venus* and Michelangelo's *David*.

2. **The Medici Dynasty**: The Medici family, often called the "Godfathers of the Renaissance," ruled Florence for centuries. Their influence extended beyond politics into art, science, and architecture, leaving an indelible mark on the city.

3. **Architectural Marvels**: Florence's skyline is a testament to its golden age. The Florence Cathedral (Duomo), designed by Filippo Brunelleschi, is a marvel of engineering and remains one of the largest domes in the world. The Palazzo Vecchio and Basilica of Santa Croce are other iconic landmarks that showcase the city's architectural prowess.

4. **Cultural Legacy**: Florence is home to some of the world's most renowned museums and galleries. The Uffizi Gallery houses an unparalleled collection of Renaissance art, while the Accademia Gallery is where you'll find Michelangelo's *David*.

5. **Literary Greats**: Florence has inspired countless writers, from Dante Alighieri, the father of the Italian

language, to modern authors like E.M. Forster, who set part of *A Room with a View* in the city.

6. **Festivals and Traditions**: Florence's culture is alive in its festivals. The annual **Scoppio del Carro** (Explosion of the Cart) during Easter and the **Calcio Storico**, a historic soccer match played in Renaissance costumes, are just a few examples of the city's vibrant traditions.

7. **Culinary Heritage**: Tuscan cuisine is simple yet deeply flavorful, rooted in the region's agricultural traditions. Dishes like pappa al pomodoro (tomato and bread soup) and cantucci (almond biscuits) are staples of Florentine tables.

Florence's history and culture are not confined to museums or textbooks—they are woven into the fabric of everyday life. As you wander its streets, you'll feel the echoes of the past mingling with the vibrant energy of the present. This is a city that celebrates its heritage while embracing the modern world, making it a truly timeless destination. 🎨🏆

Chapter 1

Planning Your Visit

Florence, the cradle of the Renaissance, is a city that captivates with its art, history, and timeless charm. Whether you're strolling across the iconic Ponte Vecchio, marveling at Michelangelo's *David*, or savoring a scoop of gelato by the Arno River, Florence promises an unforgettable experience. But before you pack your bags, a little planning can go a long way in ensuring your trip is as magical as the city itself. In this chapter, we'll help you choose the best time to visit and share budgeting tips to make your Florentine adventure both seamless and affordable.

Choosing the Best Time to Go

Florence is a year-round destination, but each season offers a unique experience. Here's a breakdown to help you decide when to visit:

- **Spring (March–May):** 🌸

  Spring is arguably the best time to visit Florence. The weather is mild (15–25°C or 59–77°F), the crowds are manageable, and the city is in full bloom. This is the perfect season for leisurely walks through the Boboli Gardens or along the Arno River. Plus, you'll catch the tail end of truffle season and the beginning of strawberry festivals in nearby Tuscan villages.

- **Summer (June–August):**

Summer in Florence is vibrant but crowded. Temperatures can soar to 35°C (95°F), so be prepared for heat. This is the peak tourist season, so expect long lines at major attractions like the Uffizi Gallery and the Duomo. However, summer evenings are magical, with open-air concerts, outdoor cinemas, and lively piazzas. If you visit in June, don't miss *Calcio Storico*, a historic football match played in Renaissance costumes.

- **Fall (September–November):**

Fall is another ideal time to visit. The summer crowds thin out, and the weather cools to a comfortable 10–25°C (50–77°F). This is harvest season in Tuscany, making it the perfect time to indulge in wine tours and truffle hunts. The golden light of autumn also makes Florence's architecture glow, creating a photographer's paradise.

- **Winter (December–February):** ❄

  Winter is the quietest and most budget-friendly time to visit. While temperatures can drop to 0°C (32°F), the city's charm remains intact. You'll find shorter lines at museums and cozy trattorias serving hearty Tuscan dishes like ribollita and bistecca alla Fiorentina. December brings festive Christmas markets and twinkling lights, adding a magical touch to the city.

Pro Tip: If you want to avoid crowds but still enjoy pleasant weather, aim for late April, May, or early October.

Trip Budgeting Tips and Tricks

Florence can be as affordable or as luxurious as you want it to be. Here's how to make the most of your budget:

1. **Accommodation:** 🏨

   - **Budget:** Hostels and budget hotels start at €20–€40 per night. Look for options in the Oltrarno district, which is quieter and more affordable than the city center.

   - **Mid-Range:** Boutique hotels and B&Bs range from €80–€150 per night. Consider

19

staying near Santa Croce or San Lorenzo for easy access to attractions.

- o **Luxury:** Splurge on a historic palazzo or a five-star hotel like the Four Seasons for €300+ per night.

2. **Food and Drink:**

   - o **Street Food:** Grab a panino from *All'Antico Vinaio* (Via dei Neri 65) for €5–€7. It's a local favorite!

   - o **Trattorias:** Enjoy a hearty Tuscan meal for €15–€25 per person at spots like *Trattoria Mario* (Via Rosina 2).

   - o **Fine Dining:** Indulge in a multi-course meal at *Enoteca Pinchiorri* (Via Ghibellina 87) for €150+ per person.

3. **Attractions:**

   - o Many museums offer free entry on the first Sunday of the month.

- Purchase the **Firenze Card** (€85) for access to over 70 museums and unlimited public transport.

- Climb the Duomo's dome (€20) for breathtaking views, or opt for the free viewing spot at Piazzale Michelangelo.

4. **Transportation:** 🚌

- Florence is a walkable city, but if you need public transport, a single bus ticket costs €1.50.

- Consider renting a bike (€10–€15 per day) to explore the city at your own pace.

5. **Shopping:** 🛍

- Skip the high-end boutiques on Via de' Tornabuoni and explore local markets like *Mercato Centrale* for affordable souvenirs, leather goods, and food.

Pro Tip: Book tickets for popular attractions like the Uffizi Gallery and Accademia Gallery online in advance to avoid long lines and secure your spot.

With the right timing and a well-planned budget, your trip to Florence will be as smooth as a glass of Chianti. In the next chapter, we'll dive into the city's top attractions and landmarks, so you can start crafting your perfect itinerary. Stay tuned!

Visa, Entry Requirements, and Documentation

Before you embark on your Florentine adventure, it's essential to ensure your travel documents are in order. Here's what you need to know:

Visa Requirements

- **EU Citizens:** No visa is required for citizens of European Union countries. A valid passport or national ID card is sufficient.

- **Non-EU Citizens:** Depending on your nationality, you may need a Schengen visa to enter Italy. The Schengen visa allows you to travel freely within 26 European countries, including Italy, for up to 90 days within a 180-day period.

- **How to Apply:** Visit the Italian consulate or embassy in your home country. You'll need to provide:

  - A completed application form

  - A valid passport (with at least six months of validity)

  - Passport-sized photos

  - Proof of travel insurance

  - Proof of accommodation and return tickets

  - Bank statements to show financial stability

- **Processing Time:** Apply at least 15–30 days before your trip, as processing can take up to two weeks.

Entry Requirements

- **Passport:** Ensure your passport is valid for at least six months beyond your planned departure date.

- **Proof of Accommodation:** Have your hotel booking or host's address ready to show at immigration.

- **Return Ticket:** Be prepared to show proof of onward travel.

- **Customs Regulations:** Familiarize yourself with Italy's customs rules. For example, you can bring up to €10,000 in cash without declaring it.

Pro Tip: Keep digital and physical copies of your passport, visa, and other important documents in case of loss or theft.

Staying Healthy and Safe: Travel Insurance, Vaccines, and Local Health Tips

Florence is a safe and welcoming city, but it's always wise to take precautions to ensure a healthy and hassle-free trip.

Travel Insurance

- **Why It's Essential:** Travel insurance covers unexpected medical expenses, trip cancellations, lost luggage, and emergencies.

- **What to Look For:**

  o Medical coverage of at least €30,000 for emergencies.

- o Coverage for COVID-19-related issues (if applicable).

- o Protection for theft or loss of personal items.

- **Recommended Providers:** World Nomads, Allianz, or AXA offer comprehensive plans for travelers.

Vaccines

- **Routine Vaccines:** Ensure you're up to date on routine vaccines like measles, mumps, rubella (MMR), and flu.

- **COVID-19:** Check Italy's current entry requirements regarding vaccinations or testing. As of 2025, proof of vaccination or a negative test may still be required.

- **Other Vaccines:** No additional vaccines are required for Florence, but consult your doctor if you plan to visit rural areas or other countries before or after your trip.

Local Health Tips

- **Pharmacies:** Look for a green cross sign (*Farmacia*). Pharmacists can provide over-the-counter medications for minor ailments.

- Example: 🛈 Farmacia Molteni (🛈 Via Calzaiuoli 7R) is centrally located and offers multilingual service.

- **Hospitals:** For emergencies, head to the nearest hospital.

  - Example: 🛈 Santa Maria Nuova Hospital (🛈 Piazza Santa Maria Nuova 1) is a trusted public hospital in Florence.

- **Tap Water:** Florence's tap water is safe to drink, so bring a reusable water bottle to stay hydrated and reduce plastic waste.

- **Sun Protection:** Summers can be scorching, so wear sunscreen, a hat, and sunglasses, especially if you're spending time outdoors.

Safety Tips

- **Pickpocketing:** Florence is generally safe, but crowded tourist areas like Piazza del Duomo and Ponte Vecchio are hotspots for pickpockets. Keep your belongings secure and avoid carrying large amounts of cash.

-

- **Emergency Numbers:**
    - 📞 112: General emergency (police, ambulance, fire)
    - 📞 118: Medical emergencies
    - 📞 113: Police
- **Night Safety:** Stick to well-lit areas and avoid walking alone late at night, especially in quieter neighborhoods.

Pro Tip: Learn a few basic Italian phrases like *"Dov'è l'ospedale?"* (Where is the hospital?) or *"Aiuto!"* (Help!) to assist in emergencies.

With your documents in order and health precautions taken care of, you're ready to explore Florence with peace of mind. In the next chapter, we'll dive into the city's top attractions and landmarks, so you can start planning your must-see list. Stay tuned!

Chapter 2

Getting to Florence

Florence, the jewel of Tuscany, is well-connected to the rest of the world, making it easy to reach no matter where you're coming from. Whether you're flying in from across the globe, taking a scenic train ride through the Italian countryside, or driving through the rolling hills of Tuscany, this chapter will guide you through the best transportation options and arrival hubs to start your Florentine adventure.

Transportation Options: Air, Land, and Sea

Florence is accessible by air, land, and even (indirectly) by sea. Here's a breakdown of your options:

1. **By Air** ✈️

Florence has its own airport, but it's relatively small. Many international travelers fly into larger airports in Italy and then take a connecting flight, train, or bus to Florence.

- **Florence Airport (FLR):** Also known as Amerigo Vespucci Airport, it's located just 6 km (4 miles) from the city center. It mainly serves domestic and European flights.

- **Pisa International Airport (PSA):** Located about 80 km (50 miles) from Florence, Pisa Airport is a popular alternative. It offers more international flights and budget airline options. From Pisa, you can take a train or bus to Florence (about 1–1.5 hours).

- **Rome Fiumicino Airport (FCO):** If you're flying from outside Europe, you'll likely land in Rome. From there, take a high-speed train to Florence (about 1.5 hours).

2. **By Train**

Italy's rail network is efficient and scenic, making trains a popular way to reach Florence.

- **High-Speed Trains:** Trenitalia's Frecciarossa and Italo trains connect Florence to major cities like Rome (1.5 hours), Milan (1.75 hours), and Venice (2 hours).

- **Regional Trains:** Slower but more affordable, regional trains are a good option for shorter distances, such as from Pisa or Bologna.

- **Florence's Main Train Station:** 🚉 Santa Maria Novella (SMN) is the city's central station, located within walking distance of many hotels and attractions.

3. **By Car** 🚗

Driving to Florence is a great option if you're exploring Tuscany or coming from nearby European countries.

- o **Highways:** Florence is connected to Italy's Autostrada network. The A1 highway links Florence to Rome, Milan, and Naples.

- o **Parking:** Parking in Florence can be challenging and expensive. Consider using a parking garage outside the city center and walking or taking public transport to your accommodation.

- o **ZTL Zones:** Be aware of Florence's *Zona a Traffico Limitato* (Limited Traffic Zones). Only residents and authorized vehicles can enter these areas, so plan your route carefully.

4. **By Bus** 🚌

Long-distance buses are a budget-friendly option for reaching Florence.

- **Major Operators:** Companies like FlixBus and MarinoBus offer routes from cities across Italy and Europe.

- **Bus Stations:** Buses typically arrive at 📍 Villa Costanza (a tram ride from the city center) or 📍 Piazza della Stazione (near Santa Maria Novella train station).

5. **By Sea** 🚢

While Florence isn't a coastal city, you can combine your trip with a Mediterranean cruise.

- **Livorno Port:** Located about 90 km (56 miles) from Florence, Livorno is a major cruise port. From here, you can take a train or bus to Florence (about 1.5 hours).

Major Airports and Arrival Hubs

Here's a closer look at the key airports and arrival hubs for Florence:

1. **Florence Airport (FLR)** 🛫

   o 📍 Location: Via del Termine, 11, 50127 Florence

   o 🕐 Hours: Open daily, 4:00 AM – 11:00 PM

   o 🖥 Website: www.aeroporto.firenze.it

   o **Getting to the City Center:**

     ▪ **Tram:** The T2 tram line connects the airport to Santa Maria Novella train station in about 20 minutes (€1.50).

     ▪ **Taxi:** A taxi ride to the city center takes about 15 minutes and costs €20–€25.

2. **Pisa International Airport (PSA)** 🛫

   o 📍 Location: Piazzale D'Ascoli, 1, 56121 Pisa

- ○ 🕐 Hours: Open daily, 4:00 AM – 12:00 AM

- ○ 🖥 Website: www.pisa-airport.com

- ○ **Getting to Florence:**

  - • **Train:** Take the PisaMover shuttle to Pisa Centrale station (5 minutes), then catch a train to Florence (1–1.5 hours, €8–€15).

  - • **Bus:** Terravision buses run directly to Florence (1.5 hours, €10).

3. **Rome Fiumicino Airport (FCO)** 🛫

- ○ 📍 Location: Via dell'Aeroporto di Fiumicino, 320, 00054 Fiumicino

- ○ 🕐 Hours: Open 24/7

- ○ 🖥 Website: www.adr.it

- ○ **Getting to Florence:**

  - • **Train:** Take the Leonardo Express to Roma Termini (30 minutes), then a high-speed train to Florence (1.5 hours, €40–€60).

34

4. **Santa Maria Novella Train Station (SMN)**

- o 📍 Location: Piazza della Stazione, 50123 Florence

- o 🕐 Hours: Open 24/7

- o 🖥 Website: www.trenitalia.com

- o **Getting to Your Accommodation:**

  - Most hotels and attractions are within walking distance. For farther destinations, use the tram or local buses.

With these transportation options and arrival hubs, getting to Florence is a breeze. In the next chapter, we'll explore the city's top attractions and landmarks, so you can start planning your itinerary. Stay tuned!

Insider Tips for Flights, Trains, and Overland Routes

Florence, the heart of Tuscany, is a well-connected destination whether you're arriving by air, rail, or road. With its rich history, breathtaking architecture, and world-class art, getting here should be as smooth as the Renaissance paintings you're about to admire! 🖼️

Flying to Florence 🛫

- Florence's main airport is:

  📍 **Amerigo Vespucci Airport (FLR)** (Peretola)

  📞 +39 055 30615

  🖥️ www.aeroporto.firenze.it

  🕐 Open 24/7

- **Best Airlines to Consider:** Major European carriers like ITA Airways, Lufthansa, and British Airways fly directly to Florence. If you're coming from outside Europe, a layover in Rome, Milan, or Frankfurt may be necessary.

- **Budget Flights:** Consider low-cost carriers like Ryanair or EasyJet, but they often land at **Pisa International Airport (PSA)** instead of Florence. Pisa is only an hour away by train.

Pro Tips for Booking Flights 💡

✅ **Best Time to Book:** Flights are cheapest when booked **2-3 months in advance** for European travelers and **4-6**

months in advance for intercontinental visitors.

✅ **Best Days to Fly:** Tuesdays and Wednesdays often have the lowest fares.

✅ **Nearby Airports for Cheaper Deals:** Check **Pisa (PSA)** or **Bologna (BLQ)** for budget options and take a train to Florence.

Arriving by Train 🚉

Florence's **Santa Maria Novella (SMN) Station** is one of Italy's busiest railway hubs. Located in the city center, it offers excellent train connections.

📍 **Santa Maria Novella Train Station (SMN)**

📞 +39 892 021

🖥 www.trenitalia.com / www.italotreno.it

🕐 Open 24/7

◆ **From Rome**: Take the **Frecciarossa high-speed train** (1.5 hours, ~€50)

◆ **From Milan**: Hop on a **Frecciarossa or Italo** train (2 hours, ~€40-€60)

◆ **From Venice**: Direct trains take about **2 hours, ~€45**

◆ **From Pisa**: Regional trains run frequently (1 hour, ~€9)

Pro Tip: 📖 **Book in advance** on Trenitalia or Italo for cheaper prices. Avoid buying tickets at the last minute, as fares can double!

Overland Routes: Buses & Road Trips

For budget travelers, long-distance buses can be an affordable alternative:

🚏 **Florence Bus Station** (near SMN Train Station)
💻 www.flixbus.it / www.itabus.it

- **From Rome**: FlixBus or Itabus (~3.5 hours, €10-€20)
- **From Milan**: FlixBus (~4.5 hours, €15-€30)
- **From Bologna**: Itabus (~1.5 hours, €5-€10)

🚗 **Driving to Florence**:

- From Rome: **A1 Autostrada**, ~3 hours
- From Milan: **A1 Autostrada**, ~3.5 hours
- From Venice: **A13 & A1 Autostrada**, ~3 hours

Pro Tip: 🚦 Florence's historic center has a **ZTL (Limited Traffic Zone)** 🚫, meaning rental cars **cannot** enter without a permit. Park at **Piazzale Michelangelo** or **Firenze Parcheggi** instead.

Arrival Guide: Customs, Transfers, and First Steps 🐿️🚗

Navigating Florence Airport (FLR) After Arrival

Once you land, follow these steps for a smooth arrival:

1 Customs & Immigration:

- **EU travelers**: No need for additional passport control if arriving from the Schengen Area.

- **Non-EU travelers**: Ensure you have your passport, visa (if needed), and proof of accommodation.

2 Luggage & Baggage Claim:

- Baggage claim is **quick** (usually under 20 minutes).

3 Getting from the Airport to the City Center:

🚗 **Taxi:** Official white taxis wait outside the terminal.

💰 Fare: ~€22-€26 (fixed rate, extra charges apply for night rides or luggage).

🚋 **Tram:** The **T2 Tram Line** connects FLR Airport to Santa Maria Novella Station.

💰 Fare: €1.50

🕐 Runs every 5-10 minutes, **6:00 AM – 12:00 AM**

🚌 **Bus:** The **Volainbus Shuttle** runs every 30 minutes.

💰 Fare: €6 one-way, €10 round-trip

Pro Tips for a Smooth Arrival

✔ **ATM & Currency Exchange:** 🏧 ATMs are available inside the airport. Exchange rates at the airport are **not the best**—withdraw euros from an ATM instead.

✔ **SIM Cards & Wi-Fi:** 📶 Get a TIM, Vodafone, or WindTre SIM at the airport (€10-€20 for data plans). Free airport Wi-Fi is available.

✔ **First Meal in Florence:** 🍲 **If you're hungry after arrival, head to** *Trattoria Mario* near SMN Station for a traditional Tuscan meal!

Chapter 3

Getting Around Florence

Florence, the jewel of Tuscany, offers a delightful mix of old-world charm and modern convenience, making it easy to navigate whether you're walking through its historic streets or hopping onto public transport. Let's dive into everything you need to know about getting around this captivating city.

Public Transport: Everything You Need to Know

Florence may be best known for its centuries-old art, architecture, and romantic atmosphere, but its public transportation system is equally modern, efficient, and user-friendly. Whether you're zipping across the city or making your way to nearby towns, the local transport options will make your travels a breeze.

Buses

Florence's extensive bus network is operated by **ATAF** and reaches nearly every corner of the city. If you plan to hop on and off throughout the day, buses are an excellent way to cover longer distances quickly.

Key Info: 📍 **Bus Stops**: You'll find bus stops throughout the city, usually marked with an "ATAF" sign. Most major tourist attractions, including the Duomo, Santa Maria Novella, and the Uffizi, are easily accessible by bus.

🕒 **Operating Hours**: Buses typically run from **5:00 AM to 12:30 AM**.

📞 **Contact**: +39 055 424 141 (ATAF Info Line)

🖥 **Website**: www.ataf.net for routes, timetables, and ticket information.

Ticket Info:

- **Single Ticket**: €1.50 (valid for 90 minutes).
- **Day Pass**: €5.00 (unlimited travel for one day).

- **Ticket Vending Machines**: Located at most bus stops and on board.

Pro Tip: For tourists, consider purchasing a **Firenze Card**, which often includes bus travel. It's a great way to save money while getting around the city, especially if you plan to visit multiple museums.

Trams

Florence also has a **tram network** that's growing in popularity. With two lines—**T1** and **T2**—the trams are a quick and comfortable way to get from one area to another, especially if you're venturing outside the historic center.

Key Info: ⚲ **Tram Stops**: Trams run between popular spots like **Santa Maria Novella** (train station), **Careggi**, and **Villa Costanza**.

🕒 **Operating Hours**: Trams operate daily from **5:00 AM to midnight**, with services running every 5-10 minutes.

📞 **Contact**: +39 055 477 7990

🖥 **Website**: www.gestram.it for route maps and timetables.

Ticket Info: The tram tickets follow the same system as buses, so the **single ticket** or **day pass** is valid for both. Just be sure to validate your ticket before boarding.

Walking

Florence is a city made for walking. The historic center is compact, pedestrian-friendly, and bursting with charm at every corner. Most of the key attractions, from the Duomo to the Ponte Vecchio, are within a short walking distance of each other. Expect to stroll down narrow cobblestone streets, past medieval buildings, and under romantic arches.

Pro Tip: Wear comfortable shoes—Florence's cobblestone streets may look picturesque, but they can be tricky on the feet. But hey, every step is part of the experience!

Taxis and Ride-Sharing

While Florence's compact nature makes walking or taking public transport convenient, there are times when you might want a little extra comfort. That's where **taxis** and **ride-sharing services** like **Uber** or **Free Now** come into play.

📍 **Taxi Stands**: You'll find them outside major attractions, train stations, and hotels. However, taxis can be difficult to hail directly from the street. It's best to head to a designated taxi stand.

🕒 **Operating Hours**: Taxis are available 24/7.

📞 **Taxi Contact**: +39 055 424 141

Pro Tip: Keep in mind that Florence's historic center has some **traffic restrictions**. Taxis can only enter certain areas, so if you're staying in the heart of the city, expect to walk a short distance from your taxi drop-off point.

Renting Cars, Scooters, and Other Vehicles

Though Florence's center is compact and best explored on foot or by public transport, you may wish to venture beyond the city for a scenic drive through the Tuscan countryside. Here's what you need to know about renting a vehicle in Florence.

Renting a Car

If you're planning to visit nearby vineyards, towns like Fiesole or San Gimignano, or even the rolling hills of Chianti, renting a car is your best bet.

Key Info: 📍 **Car Rental Locations**: Major car rental companies like **Hertz**, **Europcar**, and **Avis** have offices at **Florence Santa Maria Novella Train Station** and at **Florence Airport (Aeroporto di Firenze)**.

🕒 **Operating Hours**: Most agencies are open from **8:00 AM to 8:00 PM** (varies by company).

📞 **Contact**: Call individual rental offices for specific details.

Pro Tip: Florence's historic center has **limited access zones (ZTL)**, where cars are restricted to residents and authorized vehicles only. If you drive into one by mistake, be prepared for hefty fines. If you're only staying within the city, it's often better to leave your car parked outside the center.

Renting a Scooter or Vespa

For the ultimate Italian experience, why not rent a **Vespa** or scooter? Florence's narrow streets and scenic views make it an exciting city to navigate on two wheels.

Key Info: 📍 **Scooter Rental Locations**: Many rental shops around the city, especially near **Piazza del Duomo** and **Piazza della Signoria**, offer scooters and Vespas for rent.

🕐 **Operating Hours**: Typically **9:00 AM – 7:00 PM**, but it's best to check in advance.

📞 **Contact**: Rental shops will provide contact details when you book, but popular services include **Florence by Vespa** and **Tuscany Scooter Rental**.

Pro Tip: Florence drivers can be unpredictable, and traffic in the historic center can be intense. If you're new to riding a scooter, it's best to stick to the quieter streets or rent a bike instead.

Bicycles and E-Bikes

Florence is bike-friendly, and many visitors enjoy cycling along the **Arno River** or through the city's quieter streets. You can rent **traditional bicycles** or **e-bikes** for a fun way to explore the city at your own pace.

Key Info: 📍 **Bike Rental Locations**: Popular places like **Tuscany Bike Tours** or **Florence by Bike** offer rentals.

🕐 **Operating Hours**: **9:00 AM – 6:00 PM**, though some shops may have extended hours.

📞 **Contact**: Contact individual shops for specific rental details.

Pro Tip: E-bikes are a great choice if you want to explore more of the Tuscan hills without breaking too much of a sweat!

Whether you choose to embrace Florence's pedestrian charm or opt for the freedom of wheels, navigating the city and its surroundings is easy and enjoyable. From walking through centuries of history to cruising the rolling Tuscan hills, Florence offers a variety of transport options that fit any traveler's needs. So, what's your next adventure in this enchanting city going to be?

Walking and Cycling Routes for Explorers

Florence is a city meant to be explored on foot or by bike, where every corner holds a story, and the next alleyway is a glimpse into the past. Whether you're keen to wander through the Renaissance marvels or want to pedal through Tuscan vineyards, Florence offers a range of walking and cycling routes that reveal the best of the city and beyond.

Walking Routes for Explorers

Florence's historic center is compact, making it a perfect city for a leisurely walk. Here are a few of the most picturesque and iconic routes:

1.   The   Historic   Center   Stroll
📍 **Starting   Point**:   **Piazza   del   Duomo**
This route takes you through the heart of Florence, showcasing the city's architectural gems. Begin at the stunning **Cathedral of Santa Maria del Fiore (the Duomo)**, where you can marvel at Brunelleschi's dome. From here, head to the **Piazza della Signoria**, a true open-air museum, and walk along the **Ponte Vecchio**, the historic

49

bridge lined with shops selling gold and jewelry. You'll pass iconic landmarks like **Palazzo Vecchio**, the **Uffizi Gallery**, and the **Bargello Museum**, all the while enjoying Florence's vibrant street life.

Route Details:

- **Distance**: About 2 km (1.2 miles).

- **Duration**: 30-45 minutes of casual walking, though you'll likely want to stop and explore.

- **Pro Tip**: Start early in the morning to avoid crowds at the Duomo and the Uffizi Gallery. Don't forget to climb to the top of the Duomo for panoramic views of the city!

2. The Oltrarno District Walk

📍 **Starting Point**: **Piazza Santo Spirito**

Cross the **Ponte Santa Trinita** and explore the lesser-known but equally beautiful **Oltrarno** district, known for its artisan workshops, charming squares, and quaint streets. Wander through **Piazza Santo Spirito**, visit **Basilica di Santo Spirito**, and stroll up to **Piazzale Michelangelo** for one of the best panoramic views of Florence, especially at sunset.

Route Details:

- **Distance**: 2 km (1.2 miles).

- **Duration**: 45 minutes – 1 hour.

- **Pro Tip**: Stop by one of the local artisan workshops for handmade leather goods or enjoy an aperitivo in a cozy café near **Piazza Santo Spirito**.

3. The Boboli Gardens and Pitti Palace Walk

Starting Point: **Piazza Pitti**

This walk takes you through the stunning **Boboli Gardens**, a sprawling green oasis behind the **Pitti Palace**. Wander along tree-lined paths, admire sculptures, and enjoy the shade before heading to the **Bardini Gardens**, another picturesque spot offering a quieter experience with great views over the city.

Route Details:

- **Distance**: 1.5 km (1 mile).

- **Duration**: 1-1.5 hours, depending on how much time you spend in the gardens.

- **Pro Tip**: The gardens are best visited in spring or fall when the flowers are in bloom or the leaves are changing colors.

Cycling Routes for Explorers

For those looking to explore beyond the city center, Florence's surrounding hills and countryside offer beautiful cycling routes.

1. The Arno River Path

📍 **Starting Point: Piazza del Duomo**

For an easy and scenic bike ride, follow the path along the **Arno River**. Head west toward **Ponte Vecchio** and keep cycling along the river, passing the **Uffizi Gallery** and **Piazza della Signoria**. From here, continue west to **Cascine Park**, Florence's largest green space, where you can enjoy cycling on car-free paths.

Route Details:

- **Distance**: 5 km (3.1 miles) one way.

- **Duration**: 30-45 minutes one way.

- **Pro Tip**: The route is flat and easy for beginners, with beautiful views of Florence's riverside landmarks. If you're looking for a longer ride, head out of the city to **Fiesole**.

2. Tuscany Vineyards Cycling Tour

📍 **Starting Point**: **Piazza della Signoria**

This route takes you beyond Florence, heading towards the **Chianti** region, famous for its vineyards and rolling hills. The tour can take you along quiet roads, past rustic farmhouses, olive groves, and scenic vineyards. You'll enjoy the peaceful countryside, with opportunities to stop and visit local wineries for wine tasting.

Route Details:

- **Distance**: 30-50 km (18.6-31 miles) round trip.

- **Duration**: 3-5 hours depending on stops.

- **Pro Tip**: Rent an electric bike to make the hilly terrain of Chianti more manageable and save your energy for wine tasting!

3. Fiesole and the Tuscan Hills Ride

📍 **Starting Point: Santa Maria Novella Station**

For a challenging and rewarding ride, cycle to **Fiesole**, a hilltop town offering spectacular views of Florence. The route takes you up winding roads through cypress trees, offering fantastic panoramas. Once in Fiesole, relax and enjoy its ancient Roman amphitheater and peaceful atmosphere.

Route Details:

- **Distance**: 8 km (5 miles) one way (mostly uphill).

- **Duration**: 1.5-2 hours.

- **Pro Tip**: Start early to avoid the heat of midday and enjoy the quiet of the morning. Bring a refillable water bottle—there are fountains along the way.

Must-Have Apps for Navigation and Travel

With the right apps in hand, getting around Florence is even easier. Here are some must-have travel apps that will help you make the most of your time in this beautiful city.

1. Google Maps

For general navigation, **Google Maps** is an essential. It offers walking, cycling, and public transport directions, with real-time updates on bus and tram schedules. You can also see the walking time between landmarks, so you won't waste a moment.

Pro Tip: Download offline maps before your trip so you can navigate even without a data connection.

2. ATAF Official App

If you plan on using the bus system, the **ATAF app** is a must. It provides live updates, bus routes, and ticket information for Florence's buses and trams. You can also buy tickets directly through the app and avoid the hassle of purchasing them at machines.

3. Moovit

Moovit is another excellent public transport app, providing detailed directions for buses, trams, and even trains. It works in real-time, so you'll always know when the next bus is coming and which stop to get off at.

4. Florence by Bike

For cycling enthusiasts, this app offers cycling routes, guided bike tours, and bike rentals in and around Florence. Whether you're a beginner or a seasoned cyclist, this app will help you plan the perfect ride through Tuscany's scenic landscapes.

5. Uber or Free Now

If you prefer using ride-sharing services, **Uber** and **Free Now** operate in Florence. While taxis are readily available, these apps offer an alternative for calling a ride directly from your phone. You can easily input your destination, track your driver's arrival, and pay through the app.

6. MyTuscany

If you plan to explore the Tuscan countryside, **MyTuscany** is a great app for finding local experiences like wine tastings, hiking routes, and biking tours. It also includes a variety of walking and cycling paths that take you off the beaten path and into the heart of the Tuscan landscape.

7. Citymapper

Citymapper is ideal for navigating public transport in larger cities, and Florence is no exception. The app helps you compare multiple routes and gives live updates on when buses, trams, or trains will arrive, making it easy to plan your day.

Pro Tip: Keep your apps updated and set up an international data plan or local SIM card to avoid connection issues while traveling.

Florence offers an exceptional experience for those who love to explore on foot, by bike, or using the city's efficient public transport. Whether you're strolling past historical landmarks or cycling through the rolling hills of Tuscany, the right routes and apps will help you navigate the city with ease.

Handy Local Maps and Orientation

Florence is a city made for exploring, and getting oriented is key to making the most of your visit. Fortunately, Florence is compact and easy to navigate, so even first-time visitors can quickly feel at home. Here are some tips for getting oriented and using local maps to help you find your way around.

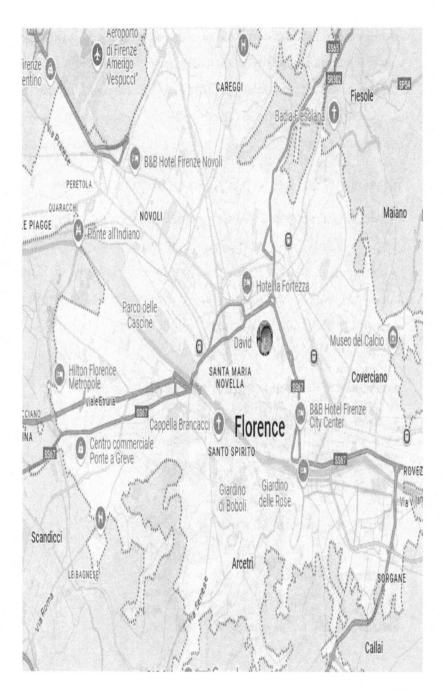

Free City Maps: When you arrive in Florence, you'll find free city maps available at most tourist information centers, including at the train station, major attractions, and hotels. These maps will highlight important landmarks, main streets, and local attractions, helping you get your bearings.

🍴 Tourist Info Locations:

- Santa Maria Novella Train Station

- Florence Airport (Amerigo Vespucci Airport)

- Piazza del Duomo (Cathedral Square) 🕐 Open: 9:00 AM – 6:00 PM daily.

Digital Maps: If you're tech-savvy and prefer digital maps, there are plenty of useful apps to download. Google Maps works perfectly in Florence and can help you get from one place to another. Additionally, apps like CityMaps2Go and Maps.me provide offline access to maps, which can be especially useful if you're not always connected to the internet.

Chapter 4

Where to Stay

Florence offers a range of accommodation options to suit all types of travelers, from those seeking luxury and indulgence to budget-conscious backpackers and families. Whether you're staying for a weekend or a week, there's a place to rest your head that will make your trip even more memorable.

Accommodation Choices: From Luxury Resorts to Cozy Budget Stays

Luxury Resorts: If you're looking to experience the best of Florence in style, the city has plenty of upscale resorts offering world-class service, elegant decor, and stunning views.

One standout is **Hotel Savoy**, a five-star hotel located just steps from the iconic Piazza della Repubblica. With its stylish rooms, fine dining options, and proximity to the city's most famous attractions, it's perfect for those who want to indulge in comfort and luxury.

📍 Location: Piazza della Repubblica 7, 50123 Florence 📞 +39 055 27370 🖥 www.roccofortehotels.com

Pro Tip: Book your stay during the off-season (October to March) to get better rates and avoid the high tourist traffic.

For an even more exclusive experience, the **Four Seasons Hotel Florence** is set in a beautiful Renaissance palace, surrounded by stunning gardens. With its spacious rooms, spa, and Michelin-star restaurant, it's ideal for those seeking the ultimate luxury getaway.

📍 Location: Borgo Pinti 99, 50121 Florence 📞 +39 055 26261 🖥 www.fourseasons.com

Mid-Range Stays: Florence also has plenty of mid-range hotels, boutique guesthouses, and charming bed-and-breakfasts for those who want comfort without breaking the bank. **Hotel Spadai**, located near the Duomo, offers spacious rooms, modern amenities, and great customer service, making it a favorite among travelers who want quality and convenience.

📍 Location: Via dei Martelli 10, 50129 Florence 📞 +39 055 277790 🖥 www.hotelspadai.com

Budget Options: For travelers looking to stretch their budget, Florence offers a variety of budget-friendly accommodations. **Plus Florence** is a great choice, offering dormitory rooms and private accommodations in a vibrant, social atmosphere. Located near the Santa Maria Novella train station, it's perfect for backpackers and solo travelers.

📍 Location: Via Santa Caterina da Siena 1, 50123 Florence 📞 +39 055 27260 🖥 www.plusflorence.com

Unique and Memorable Stays (Eco-Lodges, Treehouses, and More)

Eco-Lodges and Sustainable Stays: For travelers who are environmentally conscious, Florence has some fantastic eco-friendly accommodations that focus on sustainability. **Agriturismo Il Limoneto** offers a stay on a working organic farm just outside the city. With its peaceful setting, locally sourced meals, and eco-friendly practices, it's a great way to experience the Tuscan countryside while minimizing your carbon footprint.

📍 Location: Via della Limonaia 15, 50124 Florence 📞 +39 055 234116 🖥 www.agriturismoillimoneto.com

Pro Tip: For a more sustainable experience, consider using Florence's bike-sharing programs to explore the city in an eco-friendly way.

Treehouses and Countryside Escapes: If you're looking for something truly unique, why not try staying in a treehouse or countryside villa? Just outside the city, **Fattoria di Maiano** offers cozy treehouses and farm cottages that allow you to immerse yourself in nature without straying too far from the cultural treasures of Florence.

📍 Location: Via di Maiano 35, 50014 Fiesole, Florence 📞 +39 055 59141 🖥 www.fattoriamiano.it

Pro Tip: Treehouses are ideal for those looking to combine a peaceful retreat with proximity to Florence's museums and historic sites.

Whether you're looking for a luxurious retreat, a budget-friendly hostel, or a quirky eco-lodge, Florence offers a wide range of accommodation choices. The city's variety ensures that no matter what kind of traveler you are, there's a place that will make your stay unforgettable.

Top Neighborhoods and Areas to Stay

Florence is a city of distinct neighborhoods, each with its own personality and charm. Whether you're after a central location near major landmarks or a quieter escape in a residential area, there's something for everyone. Here are some of the top neighborhoods to stay in while visiting Florence:

Centro Storico (Historic Center):

The beating heart of Florence, the historic center is where you'll find most of the city's famous landmarks, including the Duomo, Ponte Vecchio, and the Uffizi Gallery. Staying in this area means being in the middle of the action, with plenty of cafes, shops, and museums right at your doorstep. While it can be busy and slightly more expensive, it's the best location for first-time visitors.

📍 Notable Streets: Via de' Tornabuoni, Via della Vigna Nuova 🕐 Best For: History lovers, first-time visitors, couples

Oltrarno:

Across the Arno River from the city center, Oltrarno offers

64

a more local, authentic Florence experience. This neighborhood is known for its artisan workshops, charming piazzas, and relaxed vibe. It's also home to stunning attractions like the Pitti Palace and Boboli Gardens. If you prefer staying a bit off the main tourist trail but still want to be close to the action, Oltrarno is an excellent choice.

📍 Notable Streets: Via Santo Spirito, Via de' Serragli 🕒 Best For: Art lovers, those seeking a quieter stay, foodies

Santa Croce:

This district offers a mix of historic appeal and vibrant student life. With the stunning Santa Croce Basilica and lively squares filled with cafes and restaurants, this is a fantastic neighborhood for those who want a mix of sightseeing and local culture. The area is also more affordable than staying in the city center.

📍 Notable Streets: Via dei Benci, Piazza Santa Croce 🕒 Best For: Budget travelers, history buffs, those wanting a lively atmosphere

San Lorenzo:

Home to the famous San Lorenzo Market, this area is a great spot for those who love shopping and food. The neighborhood is less touristy than the historic center but still offers proximity to key attractions like the Medici Chapels and the Florence Cathedral. It's ideal for travelers who want to be close to everything but prefer a quieter place to stay at night.

📍 Notable Streets: Via San Lorenzo, Via dei Ginori 🕐 Best For: Food lovers, shoppers, history enthusiasts

Fiesole:

For a more tranquil experience, Fiesole is a beautiful hilltop town just outside of Florence. A short bus ride or drive from the city center, Fiesole offers panoramic views of the city, ancient Roman ruins, and a peaceful atmosphere. It's perfect for travelers looking for a peaceful retreat while still being within easy reach of Florence's main attractions.

📍 Notable Streets: Via di San Francesco, Piazza Mino 🕐 Best For: Nature lovers, those seeking a peaceful escape, panoramic views

Best Picks for Families, Groups, and Solo Travelers

Families:

Florence is an incredibly family-friendly destination, offering plenty of accommodations suitable for families with children. For families, staying in **Santa Croce** or **San Lorenzo** is ideal as both neighborhoods are close to family-friendly attractions, parks, and open spaces for children to play. Hotels and apartments in these areas are generally spacious, making it easier to find family-sized rooms or multi-room apartments. Additionally, these areas are quieter in the evenings, perfect for winding down after a busy day of sightseeing.

Pro Tip: Consider booking an apartment rental for more space and flexibility, especially if you need kitchen facilities for preparing meals.

Groups:

If you're traveling with a group, **Oltrarno** is a fantastic neighborhood that offers a more laid-back vibe without sacrificing proximity to Florence's main sights. It's perfect for groups who want to explore together but also enjoy a bit of local charm. There are plenty of large apartments and guesthouses to accommodate groups, and the neighborhood's numerous restaurants and bars are great for evening hangouts.

For a more vibrant atmosphere, **Centro Storico** offers numerous hotels and Airbnbs ideal for group stays. With its central location, everyone can easily access the city's landmarks and enjoy the bustling nightlife.

Solo Travelers:

Solo travelers will love the central and walkable nature of **Centro Storico** for its convenience, allowing you to easily explore Florence's museums, churches, and hidden gems. If you're after a quieter, more reflective stay, **Fiesole** offers a peaceful retreat while being close enough to the city for day trips.

For solo adventurers looking for an authentic experience, **Oltrarno** provides a blend of local life, art, and culture with fewer crowds than the central district. You'll find plenty of cafes and local shops to explore at your own pace.

Chapter 5

Top Attractions and Landmarks

Florence is a city of unrivaled beauty, brimming with history, art, and culture. Whether you're a first-time visitor or returning for another adventure, these iconic sites and cultural landmarks are essential to your experience in the Tuscan capital. Get ready to immerse yourself in centuries of masterpieces and ancient stories that make Florence one of the world's most captivating cities.

Iconic Sites You Need to See

🗝 The Duomo (Cathedral of Santa Maria del Fiore)

No visit to Florence is complete without seeing the Duomo, a true architectural marvel. With its towering dome designed by Filippo Brunelleschi, the cathedral dominates the Florence skyline. Don't miss the chance to climb to the top for sweeping views of the city and the surrounding hills. The intricate façade, the baptistery, and the bell tower are also must-see elements of this iconic site.

🕒 Best Time to Visit: Early morning or late afternoon to avoid the crowds.

📞 +39 055 2302885

🖥 www.duomofirenze.it

📍 Piazza del Duomo, 50122 Florence

📍 **Ponte Vecchio**

The Ponte Vecchio is perhaps the most recognizable bridge in Florence. Dating back to the 14th century, it's lined with shops selling everything from gold jewelry to local artwork. Stroll along the bridge, soak in the view of the Arno River, and enjoy the centuries-old charm of this landmark. It's especially magical at sunset, with the soft glow of the sky reflecting off the water.

🕒 Best Time to Visit: Sunset for a stunning view.

📞 +39 055 2654321

🖥 www.pontevecchio.org

📍 Ponte Vecchio, Florence

📍 Uffizi Gallery

Home to some of the world's greatest works of art, the Uffizi Gallery is a must-visit for art lovers. It houses masterpieces by Botticelli, Michelangelo, Leonardo da Vinci, and Raphael. The museum is housed in a beautiful Renaissance building, and the artwork inside is just as stunning as the architecture. Be sure to book tickets in advance to skip the long lines.

🕒 Best Time to Visit: Early morning for fewer crowds.

📞 +39 055 2388651

🖥 www.uffizi.it

📍 Piazzale degli Uffizi, 6, 50122 Florence

📍 **Palazzo Pitti and Boboli Gardens**

Cross the Arno River to explore the Palazzo Pitti, a grand Renaissance palace once home to the powerful Medici family. Inside, you'll find world-class art collections, including works by Raphael and Titian. Afterward, take a peaceful stroll through the Boboli Gardens, which offer breathtaking views over Florence, fountains, sculptures, and centuries-old trees.

🕒 Best Time to Visit: Late morning to enjoy the art and gardens without the crowds.

📞 +39 055 2388612

🖥 www.uffizi.it/en/palazzo-pitti

📍 Piazza de' Pitti, 1, 50125 Florence

Cultural and Historical Highlights

📍 **Galleria dell'Accademia (Academy Gallery)** For those who are truly passionate about art, the Galleria dell'Accademia is a treasure trove of masterpieces, but it's most famous for housing Michelangelo's *David*. This awe-inspiring statue is an absolute highlight of any visit to Florence, but the gallery also features a collection of Renaissance art, musical instruments, and sculptures that'll transport you back in time.

🕐 Best Time to Visit: Midweek mornings when the gallery is less crowded.

📞 +39 055 2388609

🖥 www.accademia.org

📍 Via Ricasoli, 58/60, 50122 Florence

📍 **Piazza della Signoria**

This lively square is home to the grand Palazzo Vecchio, Florence's town hall, and is one of the most significant public spaces in the city. You'll find impressive statues here, including a replica of Michelangelo's *David*, as well as the stunning Fountain of Neptune. The square's historical importance is palpable, as it's hosted many major events throughout Florence's long and storied history.

🕐 Best Time to Visit: Late afternoon for a vibrant atmosphere.

📞 +39 055 2760330

🖥 www.museumflorence.com

📍 Piazza della Signoria, 50122 Florence

📍 Museo Nazionale del Bargello

A hidden gem, the Museo Nazionale del Bargello is an absolute must for those interested in Renaissance sculpture. Housed in a former prison, this museum showcases works by Donatello, Michelangelo, and Verrocchio. It's a quieter alternative to the more popular Uffizi, making it ideal for those looking to dive deeper into Florence's artistic history.

🕐 Best Time to Visit: Afternoon for a more peaceful experience.

📞 +39 055 2388601

🖥 www.bargellomuseum.it

📍 Via del Proconsolo, 4, 50122 Florence

📍 Basilica di Santa Croce

The Basilica di Santa Croce is not just a beautiful church, but also a mausoleum for some of Italy's greatest minds, including Galileo, Michelangelo, and Machiavelli. The church itself is a stunning example of Italian Gothic architecture, and it houses impressive frescoes by Giotto, making it one of the most important religious sites in the city.

🕐 Best Time to Visit: Early morning to avoid crowds.

📞 +39 055 2466105

🖥 www.santacroceopera.it

📍 Piazza di Santa Croce, 16, 50122 Florence

Florence is a city where every corner tells a story, and these top attractions offer a deep dive into the city's rich cultural and artistic history. Whether you're admiring the beauty of the Duomo, standing in awe before *David*, or strolling through the tranquil Boboli Gardens, you'll be immersed in the magic of one of the world's greatest cultural hubs.

Hidden Gems for Off-the-Beaten-Path Adventures

Florence is brimming with world-renowned landmarks, but the city also hides some lesser-known treasures that offer a more intimate experience of its charm. These off-the-beaten-path spots let you explore Florence like a local, away from the crowds.

Rose Garden (Giardino delle Rose) Tucked away just below Piazzale Michelangelo, the Rose Garden offers breathtaking views over Florence and a serene escape from the city's hustle. This tranquil garden is home to a stunning collection of roses, sculptures, and a peaceful atmosphere. It's the perfect spot to relax, read a book, or take a moment to appreciate the beauty of the city from a quieter vantage point.

Best Time to Visit: Late spring and early summer when the roses are in full bloom.

+39 055 2399499

www.musefirenze.it

Viale Giuseppe Poggi, 2, 50125 Florence

San Miniato al Monte

For one of the most incredible panoramic views of Florence, head up to the San Miniato al Monte church. Situated on a hilltop, this Romanesque church offers a peaceful atmosphere and a chance to escape the crowds. The view from the church's terrace is one of the best in the city, overlooking Florence with the hills and countryside in the distance. It's a bit of a walk up, but well worth the effort.

🕐 Best Time to Visit: Early morning or sunset for the most stunning views.

📞 +39 055 2342731

🖥 www.sanminiatoperfirenze.it

📍 Via delle Porte Sante, 34, 50125 Florence

📍 Officina Profumo-Farmaceutica di Santa Maria Novella

This hidden gem is a centuries-old pharmacy and perfumery, tucked away in the heart of Florence. Established in 1221 by Dominican monks, it's one of the oldest pharmacies in the world. The beautifully preserved space is a time capsule of the past, offering a range of luxurious perfumes, soaps, and herbal remedies. Visitors can take a guided tour to learn about its fascinating history and explore the stunning baroque-style rooms.

🕐 Best Time to Visit: Mid-morning, as the shop can get crowded in the afternoon.

📞 +39 055 216276

🖥 www.smnovella.com

📍 Via della Scala, 16, 50123 Florence

🏺 The Stibbert Museum

Nestled in a quiet part of the city, the Stibbert Museum is a treasure trove of armor, weaponry, and art. The museum is housed in an elegant villa, and its impressive collection includes over 50,000 pieces of historical armor and weapons from various periods and regions, making it one of the most unique museums in Florence. It's a fascinating and often overlooked stop for history buffs and those looking for something different.

🕐 Best Time to Visit: Weekdays, as weekends can be busier with local visitors.

📞 +39 055 475520

🖥 www.stibbert.it

🏺 Via Stibbert, 26, 50134 Florence

Best Spots for Photography and Scenic Views

Florence is a photographer's dream, with picturesque landscapes, stunning architecture, and vibrant street scenes at every turn. If you're looking for the best spots to capture the essence of the city, here are some top recommendations:

📍 Piazzale Michelangelo

For iconic views of Florence, head to Piazzale Michelangelo, a large square located on a hill just south of the Arno River. This is the best spot to capture a panoramic shot of Florence, with the Duomo, Ponte Vecchio, and Palazzo Vecchio all in frame. It's especially magical at sunrise or sunset when the city's golden rooftops are bathed in soft light.

🕒 Best Time to Visit: Sunset for the best lighting.

📍 Piazzale Michelangelo, 50125 Florence

📍 Boboli Gardens

While Boboli Gardens is known for its beauty and peacefulness, it also offers some fantastic spots for photography. The gardens are dotted with fountains, sculptures, and lush greenery, all set against the backdrop of the majestic Palazzo Pitti. Climb to the top of the gardens for a spectacular view of Florence and the rolling hills beyond.

🕒 Best Time to Visit: Early morning when the gardens are less crowded.

📍 Palazzo Pitti, 50125 Florence

📍 The Arno River and Ponte Vecchio

For a classic shot of Florence, nothing beats a photo of the Ponte Vecchio with the Arno River in the foreground. Whether you're standing on the bridge or looking at it from one of the nearby viewpoints, this view is quintessential Florence. The reflection of the colorful buildings in the river during the golden hour makes for stunning photography.

🕒 Best Time to Visit: Sunset for the best lighting and reflections.

📍 Ponte Vecchio, Florence

📍 San Miniato al Monte

In addition to its historical significance, San Miniato al Monte is an excellent spot for photography. The church's terrace offers one of the best panoramic views of Florence, particularly stunning at sunset. Capture the city's skyline with the Duomo rising majestically in the distance, framed by the rolling hills of Tuscany.

🕒 Best Time to Visit: Golden hour for a magical glow over the city.

📍 Via delle Porte Sante, 34, 50125 Florence

📍 Santa Croce Square

This lively square is a great place to photograph the beauty of both the architecture and the people of Florence. With the magnificent Basilica of Santa Croce as its centerpiece, this spot offers a blend of history, culture, and vibrant local life. You can often catch musicians, artists, and street performers here, adding a dynamic element to your photos.

🕒 Best Time to Visit: Late afternoon for a mix of sunlight and lively street scenes.

📍 Piazza Santa Croce, 50122 Florence

Florence is packed with hidden gems and scenic spots that offer the perfect backdrop for your photography and exploration. From the quiet beauty of San Miniato al Monte to the lively energy of Ponte Vecchio, there's no shortage of stunning places to discover and capture.

Fun and Memorable Family-Friendly Attractions

Florence isn't just for art lovers and history buffs—it's also a fantastic destination for families. With a rich mix of interactive museums, outdoor spaces, and unique experiences, there's something for everyone, including younger travelers. If you're visiting with kids, here are some of the best family-friendly attractions in the city:

📍 Florence Children's Museum (Museo dei Ragazzi)

Located within the Palazzo Vecchio, the Florence Children's Museum is a great way to introduce kids to the city's rich history in an interactive way. The museum features fun, hands-on exhibits where children can explore Florence's past through games, puzzles, and activities designed just for them. It's perfect for sparking their curiosity while keeping them entertained.

🕐 Best Time to Visit: Morning hours for a quieter experience.

📞 +39 055 2768224

🖥 www.musefirenze.it

📍 Palazzo Vecchio, Piazza della Signoria, 50122 Florence

📍 Boboli Gardens

The Boboli Gardens, located behind the Palazzo Pitti, is a great family outing. Not only are the gardens beautiful to stroll through, but they also have plenty of space for kids to run around and explore. You'll find fountains, sculptures, and hidden paths that lead to lovely viewpoints over the city. Pack a picnic, and enjoy a relaxing afternoon in one of Florence's most serene spots.

🕐 Best Time to Visit: Early morning or late afternoon to avoid peak crowds.

📞 +39 055 2388612

🖥 www.uffizi.it/en/palazzo-pitti

📍 Palazzo Pitti, 50125 Florence

📍 The Museum of the History of Science (Museo Galileo)

The Museo Galileo is a fascinating museum for kids who are curious about science and technology. It showcases the incredible inventions and discoveries made by great minds such as Galileo Galilei. From telescopes to early scientific instruments, the museum's interactive displays make learning fun. It's an educational experience that is sure to spark the imagination of kids and adults alike.

🕐 Best Time to Visit: Weekdays, especially in the mornings.

📞 +39 055 265311

🖥 www.museogalileo.it

📍 Piazza dei Giudici 1, 50122 Florence

📍 **Zoo di Firenze (Florence Zoo)**

Located a little outside the city center, the Florence Zoo is a great day trip for families with younger children. The zoo houses a variety of animals, including lions, monkeys, and elephants, and offers fun activities and educational programs. The zoo is small, making it perfect for a few hours of exploration, and it provides an opportunity for kids to learn about wildlife in a relaxed, engaging environment.

🕐 Best Time to Visit: Mid-morning, when the animals are most active.

📞 +39 055 4242060

🖥 www.zoofirenze.it

📍 Via di Castelnuovo, 50142 Florence

📍 **Parco delle Cascine (Cascine Park)**
If your kids need to burn off some energy, head to **Parco delle Cascine**, Florence's largest park. This green oasis

along the Arno River offers plenty of space for picnics, bike rides, and nature walks. There's also a playground, a small pond, and plenty of open fields for games, making it the perfect spot for families to enjoy the outdoors. In the summer months, the park hosts a weekly open-air market, which is a fun bonus!

🕐 Best Time to Visit: Late afternoon for a relaxing stroll.

📞 +39 055 328262

📍 Parco delle Cascine, 50144 Florence

📍 Leonardo da Vinci Museum

This museum is dedicated to the incredible inventions and works of Leonardo da Vinci, offering an exciting hands-on experience for children. From interactive exhibits to models of da Vinci's machines and inventions, kids will have fun learning about the genius behind some of history's most famous innovations. It's both educational and entertaining for children of all ages.

🕐 Best Time to Visit: Weekdays, ideally in the afternoon.

📞 +39 055 219432

🖥 www.museumleonardodavinci.com

📍 Via dei Servi, 66, 50122 Florence

📍 Giardino dell'ArteCultura (Art and Culture Garden)

For families with older children, the Giardino dell'ArteCultura is a wonderful spot that combines art, culture, and nature. It features outdoor art installations and cultural events that kids will find both exciting and inspiring. The garden also hosts various workshops and educational programs, so it's a fantastic option for kids who want to engage more deeply with art and creativity in a unique setting.

🕐 Best Time to Visit: Throughout the day, especially during weekend events.

📞 +39 055 625118

🖥 www.giardinoartecultura.it

📍 Via di S. Salvi 12, 50135 Florence

Florence offers a variety of family-friendly activities that allow you to dive into the city's culture while keeping younger visitors entertained. Whether it's exploring a historic museum, wandering through lush gardens, or having fun at the zoo, there's no shortage of memorable experiences for families of all ages.

Chapter 6

Things to Do: Activities and Experiences

Florence is not only a city of history and art but also one where you can enjoy a wide range of activities and experiences. Whether you're a nature enthusiast looking for outdoor adventures or a culture seeker keen on exploring the city's hidden corners, Florence offers something exciting for every traveler. Here's a mix of activities that will let you experience Florence in an unforgettable way.

Outdoor Adventures (Hiking, Diving, Ziplining, and More)

🍽 Hiking in the Tuscan Hills

Florence is surrounded by the stunning Tuscan countryside, making it a perfect base for outdoor enthusiasts. For hikers, there are plenty of trails that lead through olive groves, vineyards, and scenic hilltops offering breathtaking views of the city and surrounding villages. The **Fiesole Hills**, just a short drive from the city, offer some of the best trails with views of Florence below. The **Via degli Dei** (Way of the Gods) is a fantastic long-distance trail connecting Florence

87

to Bologna, offering incredible nature and panoramic vistas along the way.

- 🕐 Best Time to Visit: Spring and fall for mild weather and beautiful landscapes.

- 📍 Starting Point: Fiesole, just outside Florence.

- 📞 Local hiking tours: +39 055 229887

📍 Cycling in the Chianti Region

Another great way to explore the Tuscan countryside is by bike. The **Chianti region,** famous for its rolling hills and vineyards, offers scenic cycling routes suitable for all levels. Many bike tours are available from Florence, taking you through charming villages, past olive groves, and alongside picturesque vineyards. This is a great option for a full-day adventure, and it includes the chance to stop at local wineries for tastings.

- 🕐 Best Time to Visit: Late spring to early autumn for comfortable weather.

- 📞 Cycling Tours: +39 055 264 5152

- 🖥 www.tuscanybiketours.com

- 📍 Starting Point: Florence city center.

🎈 Hot Air Balloon Ride Over Tuscany

For a truly unforgettable experience, consider a hot air balloon ride over the Tuscan countryside. You'll drift high above the rolling hills, vineyards, and olive groves as you take in panoramic views of Florence and beyond. Many tours offer sunrise rides, providing a magical experience as the morning light bathes the landscape in a soft glow.

- 🕐 Best Time to Visit: Sunrise for the most picturesque lighting.

- 📞 Balloon Tours: +39 055 5010920

- 🖥 www.flytuscany.com

- 🎈 Departing from various points in Tuscany.

🎈 Ziplining in Tuscany

If you're looking for something a bit more thrilling, head to **Tuscany Zip Line**, located near the town of Pescia. This adventure park offers a range of zipline courses through the lush forest, with incredible views of the surrounding mountains. It's an adrenaline-packed activity that's sure to get your heart racing while allowing you to take in the beauty of the region from above.

- 🕐 Best Time to Visit: Morning for cooler temperatures and quieter crowds.

- 📞 +39 0583 622130

- 🖥 www.tuscanyzipline.com

- 📍 Via del Cerro, 51017 Pescia, Tuscany.

Neighborhood Strolls and Guided Tours

📍 Walking Tour of Florence's Historic Center

The best way to get to know Florence is on foot, and there's no shortage of walking tours that take you through the city's most iconic and charming neighborhoods. Many guided tours cover landmarks such as the **Duomo**, **Piazza della Signoria**, and the **Uffizi Gallery**, but some also delve deeper into hidden gems and local history. A guided walking tour will give you insider knowledge, including stories behind famous art pieces and the fascinating history of Florence.

- 🕐 Best Time to Visit: Early morning or late afternoon to avoid crowds.

- 📞 Walking Tours: +39 055 290683

- 🖥 www.walkaboutflorence.com

- 📍 Starting point: Piazza della Signoria.

📍 Oltrarno District Tour

If you're looking for something less touristy, take a guided tour of **Oltrarno**, the artistic district on the other side of the Arno River. Known for its artisan workshops, cozy cafes, and hidden treasures, this neighborhood offers a more local, off-the-beaten-path feel. A walking tour will take you through narrow streets, past historic churches, and into the studios of local craftsmen.

- 🕐 Best Time to Visit: Late morning for a peaceful walk.

- 📞 Oltrarno Tours: +39 055 265311

- 🖥 www.olfatrontour.com

- 📍 Starting point: Santo Spirito Square.

📍 Food Tour in the San Lorenzo Market

Food lovers will delight in a **San Lorenzo Market food tour**. This bustling market is filled with fresh produce, meats, cheeses, and Tuscan specialties. A local guide will take you through the market, providing insights into local food culture, and introducing you to various tastings along the way. You'll get to try delicious local cheeses, cured meats, and maybe even a slice of classic Florentine steak.

- 🕐 Best Time to Visit: Mid-morning for fewer crowds.

- 📞 Food Tours: +39 055 213768

- 🖥 www.tasteflorence.com

- 📍 Location: Piazza San Lorenzo.

📍 Art and History Tour of the Uffizi Gallery

If you're keen on diving deep into Florence's art history, a guided tour of the **Uffizi Gallery** is a must. The museum is home to some of the world's greatest masterpieces, including Botticelli's *The Birth of Venus* and da Vinci's *Annunciation*. An expert guide will walk you through the museum, explaining the historical context of the artwork and sharing fascinating stories behind each piece.

- 🕐 Best Time to Visit: Early morning for a quieter experience.

- 📞 Uffizi Gallery Tours: +39 055 2388651

- 🖥 www.uffizi.it

- 📍 Piazzale degli Uffizi, 6, 50122 Florence.

Florence offers an incredible variety of activities to suit all kinds of adventurers, from outdoor thrill-seekers to culture lovers. Whether you're hiking through the Tuscan hills, taking a walking tour through the heart of the city, or indulging in a local food experience, these activities and experiences will make your trip to Florence unforgettable.

Local Experiences: Cooking, Crafting, and Cultural Immersion

Florence is not just about admiring art and exploring historical sites—it's also a city where you can truly immerse yourself in the local culture. Whether it's cooking a traditional Tuscan meal, learning the art of crafting, or experiencing Florence through the eyes of its residents, here are some unforgettable local experiences to add to your itinerary.

📍 **Cooking Class: Learn the Secrets of Tuscan Cuisine**

What better way to experience the heart of Florence than by learning how to prepare some of the region's most iconic dishes? A cooking class will teach you how to create traditional Tuscan meals using fresh, local ingredients. Popular classes include making *pasta fresca*, *ragu*, and *tiramisu*. Afterward, you'll get to enjoy your creations with a glass of Chianti wine, sharing your meal with fellow food lovers.

- 🕒 Best Time to Visit: Mid-morning classes for a relaxed experience.

- 📞 Cooking School: +39 055 2670477

- 🖥 www.italian-cooking-class.com

- 📍 Location: Various venues across Florence.

📍 Leather Crafting Workshop

Florence has been a hub of leather production for centuries, and a hands-on leather crafting workshop is a unique way to connect with the city's long-standing artisan traditions. You'll learn how to make your own leather goods, such as wallets, belts, or bags, from experienced craftsmen who use time-honored techniques. It's a great way to bring home a one-of-a-kind souvenir while learning about the craftsmanship that makes Florentine leather so special.

- 🕒 Best Time to Visit: Weekdays for a more personal experience.

- 📞 Leather Workshop: +39 055 263658

- 🖥 www.florencecrafts.com

- 📍 Location: Near Santa Croce district.

📍 **Wine Tasting and Vineyard Tour**

No visit to Tuscany is complete without experiencing its world-famous wines. Join a vineyard tour just outside Florence to explore the rolling hills of Chianti, where you'll learn about the winemaking process and taste local varieties. Many tours also include a light lunch of Tuscan specialties, making it a perfect way to spend a relaxing afternoon in the countryside.

- 🕐 Best Time to Visit: Late spring or early autumn for harvest season.

- 📞 Wine Tours: +39 055 2342424

- 🖥 www.chiantiwine.com

- 📍 Starting from Florence city center.

Seasonal Highlights: Festivals, Events, and Activities

Florence offers an exciting array of events and activities throughout the year, making it an appealing destination no matter when you visit. Whether you're here to experience a cultural celebration, enjoy outdoor festivals, or take part in seasonal traditions, there's always something to look forward to.

📍 Festa della Rificolona (Festival of the Lanterns) Held every September 7th, this colorful festival celebrates the Feast of the Nativity of the Virgin Mary. Children and families light up the streets with colorful lanterns, parading through the city with music and festivities. The evening culminates in a grand celebration in Piazza Santa Croce, where locals and visitors come together for a night of food, dancing, and fun.

- 🕐 Best Time to Visit: September 7th for the full festival experience.

- 📍 Piazza Santa Croce and surrounding streets.

📍 Maggio Musicale Fiorentino (Florence Musical May Festival)

This prestigious annual event, held every spring, showcases a wide range of performances from classical music, opera, ballet, and contemporary theatre. If you're a fan of the arts, attending one of the world-class performances during the **Maggio Musicale Fiorentino** is an unforgettable way to experience Florence's cultural scene.

- 🕐 Best Time to Visit: May for the full festival experience.

- 📞 +39 055 2768424

- 🖥 www.maggiofiorentino.com

- 📍 Teatro del Maggio Musicale Fiorentino.

📍 **Pitti Immagine Uomo (Florence Men's Fashion Week)**

Fashion lovers, take note! Florence hosts one of the most important events in the global fashion calendar: **Pitti Immagine Uomo**. Held twice a year, this event brings together the best of men's fashion from around the world, with runway shows, exhibitions, and exclusive presentations. Even if you're not a fashion expert, the buzz around this event and the stylish crowd it attracts make it a fun and exciting time to visit Florence.

- 🕐 Best Time to Visit: January and June for the event's main shows.

- 📞 +39 055 3693323

- 🖥 www.pittimmagine.com

- 📍 Fortezza da Basso.

📍 Winter in Florence: Ice Skating and Christmas Markets

Florence transforms into a magical winter wonderland during the holiday season. From late November to early January, the city hosts various Christmas markets, where you can shop for unique gifts, enjoy seasonal treats, and sip hot mulled wine. The **Piazza Santa Croce** market is one of the most popular, offering handcrafted goods and festive food. You can also enjoy ice skating at the temporary rink set up in the city center, which is a fun way for families and friends to enjoy the winter months.

- 🕐 Best Time to Visit: Late November through December for festive activities.

- 📍 Piazza Santa Croce for the Christmas market and ice rink.

♟ Calcio Storico (Historic Florentine Football)

If you're visiting Florence in June, don't miss **Calcio Storico**, a traditional game dating back to the 16th century. Played in the Piazza Santa Croce, this intense and dramatic game combines soccer, rugby, and wrestling. It's a thrilling spectacle that draws large crowds, and it's one of the most exciting events to witness in Florence. The match is held on **June 24th**, in celebration of Florence's patron saint, St. John the Baptist.

- 🕐 Best Time to Visit: June 24th for the full experience.

- ♟ Piazza Santa Croce.

Florence's seasonal highlights and local experiences give you the chance to connect with the city in a deeper, more immersive way. From the music and artistry of festivals to the hands-on joys of cooking and crafting, there's no shortage of activities to make your trip uniquely memorable.

Nature and Wildlife Adventures

While Florence is famous for its art and history, the surrounding Tuscan countryside offers a treasure trove of natural beauty and wildlife adventures. From exploring serene parks to spotting local wildlife, here's how to enjoy the outdoors and experience Tuscany's natural wonders.

📍 Florence Botanical Garden (Giardino dei Semplici)

Located in the heart of Florence, the **Florence Botanical Garden** is one of the oldest botanical gardens in Italy. This peaceful haven is the perfect place to unwind while surrounded by centuries-old trees, colorful flowers, and exotic plants. The garden features a variety of plant species, including medicinal herbs, and offers educational workshops on botany and conservation. It's an ideal spot for nature lovers and anyone looking to escape the city's hustle and bustle.

- 🕐 Best Time to Visit: Early morning or late afternoon for a quiet stroll.

- 📞 +39 055 2757707

- 🖥 www.unifi.it

- 📍 Via Pier Antonio Micheli, 26, 50121 Florence.

📍 Parco delle Cascine (Cascine Park)

As Florence's largest park, **Parco delle Cascine** is a popular spot for locals and tourists alike, offering a green oasis for outdoor activities. The park stretches along the Arno River, providing plenty of space for jogging, biking, and even horseback riding. You can also enjoy birdwatching or take a leisurely walk through its tree-lined paths. For families, there's a playground, and in the summer, the park hosts open-air concerts and festivals.

- 🕐 Best Time to Visit: Late afternoon when the weather is cooler.

- 📞 +39 055 328262

- 📍 Parco delle Cascine, 50144 Florence.

📍 The Tuscan Hills and Vineyards

Tuscany's rolling hills, dotted with vineyards and olive groves, are an iconic part of the region's landscape. You can explore these hills on foot, by bike, or even on horseback. Many tour companies offer day trips from Florence that include a hike through the countryside, followed by a visit to a local vineyard for a wine-tasting experience. The area around **Fiesole** is particularly scenic, offering views over Florence and the opportunity to spot local wildlife, such as wild boar and deer.

- 🕐 Best Time to Visit: Spring and fall for mild temperatures and stunning landscapes.

- 📞 Tuscany Tours: +39 055 2670477

- 🖥 www.tuscanybiketours.com

- 📍 Fiesole, just outside Florence.

📍 Guided Wildlife and Birdwatching Tours

Tuscany is home to a variety of wildlife, and there are several nature reserves and wildlife parks around Florence where you can spot local species. For a truly immersive experience, join a **guided birdwatching tour** or wildlife safari. **Parco di San Rossore**, located near Pisa, is a vast natural park where you can see a wide range of animals, including wild boar, deer, and over 150 species of birds. Many tours also include a visit to local farms, where you can learn about conservation efforts in the region.

- 🕐 Best Time to Visit: Early morning for the best chance to spot wildlife.

- 📞 Wildlife Tours: +39 0587 517227

- 🖥 www.parcosanrossore.org

- 📍 Parco di San Rossore, Pisa (about 1 hour from Florence).

📍 The Mugello Valley

Located just north of Florence, the **Mugello Valley** is a great destination for nature lovers seeking to explore the Tuscan wilderness. Known for its lush forests, clear lakes, and medieval villages, the valley is a perfect spot for hiking, cycling, and wildlife spotting. The area is home to several protected species, including wild boar, deer, and birds of prey. For a more adventurous experience, consider a rafting trip on the **Sieve River**, which runs through the valley.

- 🕐 Best Time to Visit: Late spring to early autumn when the weather is ideal for outdoor activities.

- 📞 Mugello Tours: +39 055 8498700

- 🖥 www.mugelloturismo.it

- 📍 Mugello Valley, 50135 Florence (about 30 minutes from the city).

📍 Nature Walks in the Casentino Forests

For those seeking more rugged adventures, head to the **Casentino Forests**, a protected nature reserve located within the **Foreste Casentinesi, Monte Falterona, and**

Campigna National Park. The park offers a variety of walking and hiking trails that wind through dense forests, rivers, and streams. Wildlife enthusiasts can spot species like wild boar, roe deer, and the rare Apennine wolf. The area is also home to ancient monasteries, making it a perfect blend of nature and history.

- 🕐 Best Time to Visit: Spring and early fall for cool weather and blooming landscapes.

- 📞 Nature Tours: +39 0575 50301

- 🖥 www.parcoforestecasentinesi.it

- 📍 Casentino Forests, 52010 Arezzo (about 1.5 hours from Florence).

Florence is surrounded by natural beauty, offering endless opportunities to explore the great outdoors and spot wildlife. Whether you're strolling through a botanical garden, hiking in the Tuscan hills, or taking a wildlife safari in a nearby park, these adventures will give you a deeper connection to the stunning landscapes of Tuscany.

Chapter 7

Food and Drink Scene

Florence is a city that delights all the senses, and its food and drink scene is no exception. From rich, hearty dishes that tell the story of Tuscany's agricultural roots to refreshing wines and creative cocktails, the city offers a feast for anyone who loves great cuisine. Whether you're a seasoned foodie or someone simply looking to try a local delicacy, here's a guide to some must-try dishes, drinks, and dining spots that span every budget.

Can't-Miss Local Dishes and Drinks

Florentine cuisine is deeply rooted in the Tuscan tradition, with an emphasis on simple, high-quality ingredients. Here are some dishes and drinks that you simply can't miss while in Florence:

Bistecca alla Fiorentina (Florentine Steak) This iconic dish is the ultimate must-try in Florence. It's a massive T-bone steak, grilled to perfection and typically served rare or medium-rare. The steak is sourced from local Chianina cattle, known for its tender, flavorful meat. Pair it with a glass of **Chianti** wine for the full Tuscan experience.

- ⏱ Best Time to Try: Dinner, as it's traditionally served as a shared dish.

- 🍴 Where to Try: Trattoria Marione, Via della Spada 27/r.

🍴 Ribollita (Tuscan Vegetable Soup)

This hearty soup is a quintessential Tuscan dish, made with seasonal vegetables, beans, and **cavolo nero** (Tuscan kale). Ribollita, meaning "re-boiled," was traditionally made with leftovers, but today it's a beloved comfort food. It's perfect for colder days, and you'll often find it served with a slice of toasted bread.

- ⏱ Best Time to Try: Fall or winter when it's cooler.

- 🍴 Where to Try: Osteria Santo Spirito, Piazza Santo Spirito 16/r.

🍴 Pappardelle al Cinghiale (Wild Boar Pappardelle)

Pappardelle is a wide, flat pasta that pairs perfectly with a rich, savory wild boar ragu. This dish is a staple of Tuscan cuisine, reflecting the region's love for game meats. It's often served with a full-bodied red wine like **Chianti Classico**.

- ⏱ Best Time to Try: Anytime for a satisfying meal.

- 🍴 Where to Try: Trattoria 4 Leoni, Via Vangelo 5r.

🍴 Lampredotto (Florentine Street Food)

For an authentic Florentine street food experience, try **lampredotto**, a sandwich made with slow-cooked beef tripe, served in a bun with salsa verde (green sauce) and sometimes hot broth. It's beloved by locals and a great snack while exploring the city.

- 🕑 Best Time to Try: Late morning to early afternoon.

- 🍴 Where to Try: La Trippaio del Porcellino, Piazza del Mercato Nuovo.

🍴 Vin Santo and Cantucci (Dessert)

End your meal with **vin santo**, a rich, sweet dessert wine traditionally paired with **cantucci** (biscotti). This simple yet satisfying combination is a perfect finish to any meal, especially if you're in the mood for something sweet but not too heavy.

- 🕑 Best Time to Try: After dinner, as a digestif.

- 🍴 Where to Try: Enoteca Pitti Gola e Cantina, Via Romana 35/r.

Best Restaurants, Cafes, and Bars for Every Budget

Florence has a thriving dining scene that caters to all types of travelers, from those seeking fine dining to budget-conscious eaters. Whether you're looking for a quick bite, a leisurely lunch, or an upscale dinner, here are some top dining spots for every budget.

🍰 Budget-Friendly

🍴 Trattoria Marione

Located in the heart of Florence, this cozy trattoria serves classic Florentine dishes at reasonable prices. From **bistecca alla fiorentina** to **pasta al ragù**, you'll find hearty meals that deliver excellent value. The atmosphere is warm and inviting, making it a great place for a casual meal.

- 📞 +39 055 212287

- 🖥 www.trattoriamarione.com

- 🍴 Via della Spada 27/r, Florence.

🍴 All' Antico Vinaio

One of the most popular sandwich spots in Florence, **All' Antico Vinaio** serves up delicious, oversized sandwiches stuffed with Tuscan meats, cheeses, and fresh ingredients. The line can get long, but the sandwiches are totally worth the wait.

- 📞 +39 055 2382723

- 🖥 www.allanticovinaio.com

- 📍 Via de' Neri, 74r, Florence.

📍 Osteria Santo Spirito

For a truly local experience, head to **Osteria Santo Spirito**, where you can enjoy traditional Tuscan dishes at affordable prices. The atmosphere is lively, and you can sit outside in Piazza Santo Spirito to enjoy the local vibe.

- 📞 +39 055 200 1695

- 🖥 www.osteriastospirito.com

- 📍 Piazza Santo Spirito 16/r, Florence.

🍽 Mid-Range

📍 Trattoria 4 Leoni

Located in the charming **Piazza della Passera, Trattoria 4 Leoni** is famous for its **pappardelle al cinghiale** and other classic Tuscan dishes. The restaurant has a cozy, rustic atmosphere and serves generous portions of freshly prepared food.

- 📞 +39 055 218562

- 🖥 www.4leoni.com

- 📍 Via Vangelo 5r, Florence.

📍 La Giostra

If you're looking for a bit of romance, **La Giostra** offers a magical ambiance with its chandeliers and cozy atmosphere. Known for its friendly service and delicious food, it's a great place to try Tuscan specialties like **tagliatelle with truffles** and **wild boar ragu**.

- 📞 +39 055 241341

- 🖥 www.ristorantelagiostra.com

- 📍 Borgo Pinti 12r, Florence.

🍷 Upscale

📍 Enoteca Pinchiorri

For a truly fine dining experience, **Enoteca Pinchiorri** is one of Florence's Michelin-starred gems. This exquisite restaurant offers innovative Italian cuisine paired with an impressive wine list. Located near the **Piazza della Signoria**, it's perfect for a special occasion or an indulgent evening.

- 📞 +39 055 242757

- 🖥 www.enotecapinchiorri.com

- 📍 Via Ghibellina 87, Florence.

📍 Il Palagio

Il Palagio, located in the luxurious **Four Seasons Hotel Florence**, offers a Michelin-starred dining experience with a focus on contemporary Italian cuisine. The elegant setting, paired with expertly crafted dishes, makes it the perfect spot for a romantic dinner or a special celebration.

- 📞 +39 055 2626450

- 🖥 www.fourseasons.com/florence/dining

- 📍 Borgo Pinti 99, 50121 Florence.

Florence's food and drink scene is a highlight of any visit. From casual street food to world-class fine dining, there's a taste for every budget. Don't miss out on the chance to experience the authentic flavors of Tuscany, whether you're indulging in a classic **bistecca alla fiorentina** or sipping a glass of **vin santo** after your meal.

Street Food, Markets, and Culinary Tours

Florence is not just for sit-down meals—its street food, bustling markets, and culinary tours are a big part of what makes the city's food scene so exciting. From savory snacks to vibrant markets, here are the best ways to dive into the local food culture on the go.

All' Antico Vinaio

No visit to Florence is complete without grabbing a sandwich at **All' Antico Vinaio**. Located near the **Piazza del Duomo**, this legendary sandwich shop is known for its delicious, overstuffed panini. You can fill your sandwich with a variety of meats, cheeses, and fresh vegetables, often served with a drizzle of local olive oil. Expect long lines, but the wait is absolutely worth it for this iconic street food experience.

- Best Time to Visit: Early afternoon to avoid peak crowds.

- 📞 +39 055 2382723

- 🖥 www.allanticovinaio.com

- 📍 Via de' Neri, 74r, Florence.

📍 Mercato Centrale (Central Market)

For an authentic taste of Florence's food culture, head to **Mercato Centrale**, Florence's bustling indoor market. Here, you'll find fresh produce, meats, cheeses, and ready-to-eat meals like **porchetta sandwiches** and **pasta with ragu**. The top floor of the market also has several eateries offering local specialties and seating for a more leisurely meal. It's the perfect place to sample a bit of everything.

- 🕐 Best Time to Visit: Late morning for a quieter experience.

- 📞 +39 055 2399798

- 🖥 www.mercatocentrale.it

- 📍 Piazza del Mercato Centrale, 50123 Florence.

📍 Street Food Tours

If you want to sample the best of Florence's street food scene, consider taking a **food tour**. A guided walking tour takes you through Florence's narrow streets and vibrant neighborhoods, stopping at food stalls and local eateries along the way. You'll taste **lampredotto** (a sandwich with beef tripe), **crostini di fegatini** (chicken liver pâté), and much more while learning about the history behind these beloved Florentine treats.

- 🕐 Best Time to Visit: Morning or afternoon for a relaxed pace.

- 📞 +39 055 213768

- 🖥 www.tasteflorence.com

- 📍 Various locations throughout Florence.

Cooking Classes and Foodie Experiences

For anyone wanting to take home more than just a taste of Florence, a cooking class or foodie experience is a fantastic way to dive deeper into Tuscan cuisine. These experiences allow you to learn local techniques, discover new flavors, and bring some of the magic back home.

📍 **Cooking Classes in Florence**
Florence offers a variety of cooking classes, where you can

learn how to make classic Tuscan dishes like **pasta fresca** (fresh pasta) and **ragu** from scratch. Local chefs teach you the secrets of Italian cooking, using fresh, seasonal ingredients. At the end of the class, you'll sit down to enjoy the meal you've prepared, often paired with local wines.

- 🕐 Best Time to Visit: Mid-morning for a relaxing, hands-on class.

- 📞 Cooking School: +39 055 2670477

- 🖥 www.italian-cooking-class.com

- 📍 Various venues across Florence.

📍 Tuscan Wine and Food Tour

For food and wine lovers, a **Tuscan wine and food tour** is a must-do. This experience combines a guided visit to local wineries with food pairings and tastings of regional specialties. You'll visit vineyards in the **Chianti region**, where you'll learn about the winemaking process, sample some of Tuscany's best wines, and enjoy a delicious lunch with local cheeses, meats, and fresh bread.

- 🕐 Best Time to Visit: Spring and fall for ideal weather and harvest season.

- 📞 Wine Tours: +39 055 2342424

- 🖥 www.chiantiwine.com

- 📍 Departing from Florence.

📍 Pasta-Making Classes

If pasta is your favorite part of any Italian meal, a **pasta-making class** in Florence will show you the art of creating fresh pasta from scratch. In these classes, you'll learn how to make everything from delicate ravioli to hearty pappardelle, all while picking up tips and tricks from expert chefs. The best part? You'll enjoy your creations with a glass of local wine at the end of the class.

- 🕐 Best Time to Visit: Morning or early afternoon for a leisurely class.

- 📞 Pasta School: +39 055 282010

- 🖥 www.florencecookingschool.com

- 📍 Location: Near the city center.

📍 Market Tour and Cooking Class

For those who want a truly immersive experience, a **market tour and cooking class** combines the best of Florence's culinary offerings. You'll visit the famous **Mercato Centrale** to shop for fresh, local ingredients with your guide, then head to a local kitchen to learn how to prepare traditional dishes. It's a hands-on way to learn about Tuscan flavors and cooking techniques, all while exploring the city's vibrant food scene.

- 🕐 Best Time to Visit: Midday for an exciting mix of shopping and cooking.

- 📞 Market Tours: +39 055 242734

- 🖥 www.flavorsofitaly.com

- 📍 Mercato Centrale and various kitchens.

Florence's food scene is an adventure in itself, and these experiences allow you to immerse yourself fully in the culture and flavors of Tuscany. From savoring street food to learning the art of Italian cooking, these culinary tours and classes will leave you with unforgettable memories—and the skills to recreate them at home.

Chapter 8

Cultural Insights

Florence is a city rich in history, art, and traditions, and understanding the local customs and etiquette will help you connect with the city and its people on a deeper level. Whether it's knowing how to greet someone or understanding the etiquette at the dinner table, embracing Florence's cultural nuances will enhance your experience.

Local Customs, Traditions, and Etiquette

1. Greetings and Politeness

In Florence, as in the rest of Italy, greetings are important. Italians value personal connection, and a polite greeting sets the tone for any interaction. Here's what you should know:

- **Ciao** is the most common greeting, used with friends and people of your age. However, it's important to note that this informal greeting isn't used in more formal settings or with strangers.

- **Buongiorno** (Good morning) and **Buonasera** (Good evening) are used in more formal situations and with people you don't know well.

118

- **Arrivederci** (Goodbye) or **A presto** (See you soon) are polite ways to leave.

Italians tend to greet each other with a firm handshake, but when you get to know someone better, a kiss on both cheeks (starting with the left) is common among close friends and family.

2. Dining Etiquette

Food is an integral part of Florentine culture, and understanding the local dining etiquette is essential for a smooth experience. Here are a few tips:

- **Punctuality**: Being on time for dinner is important, especially in formal restaurants. However, lunch hours can be more relaxed, with many restaurants opening late (between 12:30 PM and 1:00 PM) and closing for a break between 3:00 PM and 7:00 PM.

- **Order of Courses**: A typical meal in Florence starts with an appetizer, followed by pasta, a meat dish, and dessert. You may also be served an intermezzo (a small palate cleanser) between courses.

- **Table Manners**: Keep your hands visible on the table (but not your elbows) and avoid using your phone during meals. It's polite to wait for the host to begin eating before you do.

- **Coffee**: In Italy, coffee is often consumed in the morning or after meals. The most common coffee drinks are espresso (served in a small cup) and cappuccino (served in the morning, never after a meal). Italians don't typically drink coffee with meals, so avoid ordering a cappuccino at dinner.

3. Dress Code

Florence has a refined sense of style, and while it's not as formal as some other Italian cities, it's always good to dress neatly. Italians tend to dress up even for casual outings, so you may feel out of place if you're wearing overly casual attire, especially when dining at nice restaurants. Keep in mind:

- **Churches and Religious Sites**: When visiting churches or religious sites like the **Duomo** or **Basilica di Santa Croce**, be sure to dress modestly. Shoulders and knees should be covered, and hats should be removed.

- **Day-to-Day**: Florence is a fashionable city, so avoid wearing overly casual clothing like flip-flops or sweatpants in public places. Opt for smart-casual attire, especially in the evening.

4. Tipping

Tipping in Italy is appreciated but not mandatory. In restaurants, service is typically included in the bill, but it's polite to leave small change (around 5-10%) or round up the bill for excellent service. Similarly, for taxi rides, rounding up the fare is a common practice.

Phrases to Know in the Local Language

While many people in Florence speak English, especially in tourist areas, learning a few key Italian phrases will enhance your experience and show respect for the local culture. Here are some helpful phrases to know:

Basic Greetings and Phrases

- **Ciao** – Hi / Bye (informal)

- **Buongiorno** – Good morning

- **Buonasera** – Good evening

- **Arrivederci** – Goodbye

- **Come stai?** – How are you? (informal)

- **Sto bene, grazie** – I'm good, thank you

- **Mi scusi** – Excuse me (polite)

- **Per favore** – Please

- **Grazie** – Thank you

- **Prego** – You're welcome

In Restaurants and Cafes

- **Un tavolo per [due] persone, per favore** – A table for [two], please

- **Il conto, per favore** – The check, please

- **Acqua naturale / frizzante** – Still water / sparkling water

- **Vino rosso / bianco** – Red wine / white wine

- **Caffè** – Coffee (espresso)

- **Un cappuccino** – A cappuccino

Asking for Directions

- **Dove si trova [il Duomo]?** – Where is [the Duomo]?

- **Come arrivo a [Piazza della Signoria]?** – How do I get to [Piazza della Signoria]?

- **È lontano?** – Is it far?

- **A destra / a sinistra** – To the right / to the left

Shopping and Sightseeing

- **Quanto costa?** – How much does it cost?

- **Posso pagare con la carta di credito?** – Can I pay with a credit card?

- **Mi può aiutare?** – Can you help me?

- **Vorrei comprare [un souvenir]** – I would like to buy [a souvenir]

Understanding and respecting the local customs and learning a few key phrases will make your time in Florence even more enjoyable. It will also allow you to connect more authentically with the people you meet along the way.

Festivals, Celebrations, and Holidays to Plan Around

Florence is a city that comes alive with festivals, celebrations, and holidays throughout the year. Each one offers a unique opportunity to experience the city's culture and traditions. Here are some of the top events you might want to plan your trip around.

📍 Festa della Rificolona (Festival of the Lanterns)

Held annually on **September 7th**, this festival celebrates the Feast of the Nativity of the Virgin Mary. The city is filled with children carrying brightly lit lanterns, parading through the streets and culminating in a celebration in **Piazza Santa Croce**. It's a fun and colorful event, especially for families, and offers a glimpse into Florence's local traditions.

- 🕐 Best Time to Visit: September 7th.

- 📍 Piazza Santa Croce.

📍 Calcio Storico (Historic Florentine Football)

For those seeking a thrilling experience, the **Calcio Storico** (Historic Florentine Football) is an event that shouldn't be missed. Held every year on **June 24th** in **Piazza Santa Croce**, this ancient game is a blend of soccer, rugby, and wrestling. It's a high-energy event that draws huge crowds, and the atmosphere is intense as the four historic districts of Florence compete for victory.

- 🕐 Best Time to Visit: June 24th.

- 📍 Piazza Santa Croce.

📍 Maggio Musicale Fiorentino (Florence Musical May Festival)

Every spring, Florence hosts the **Maggio Musicale Fiorentino**, one of Italy's most prestigious arts festivals, which runs through the month of May. The festival includes opera, classical music concerts, ballet, and theater performances held at the **Teatro del Maggio Musicale Fiorentino**. If you're a fan of the arts, this is one of the city's most exciting cultural events.

- 🕐 Best Time to Visit: May.

- 📍 Teatro del Maggio Musicale Fiorentino.

📍 **Pitti Immagine Uomo (Florence Men's Fashion Week)**
Fashion enthusiasts will appreciate Florence's **Pitti Immagine Uomo**, one of the most important events on the international fashion calendar. Held twice a year in **January** and **June**, this men's fashion week showcases the latest trends from the world's leading designers. The event is an exciting blend of runway shows, exhibitions, and presentations, with a stylish crowd making it one of the most fashionable times to visit the city.

- 🕐 Best Time to Visit: January and June.

- 📍 Fortezza da Basso.

📍 Christmas Markets and Winter Celebrations

Florence transforms into a festive wonderland during the holiday season. From late November through early January, Christmas markets fill the squares, offering local crafts, holiday treats, and mulled wine. One of the most popular markets is in **Piazza Santa Croce**, where you can shop for unique gifts, enjoy festive music, and sip hot chocolate. Ice skating rinks also pop up in various parts of the city, providing fun for all ages.

- 🕐 Best Time to Visit: Late November to December for holiday festivities.

- 📍 Piazza Santa Croce.

Exploring Local Art, Music, and Performances

Florence is world-renowned for its artistic legacy, and there's no better way to immerse yourself in the city's cultural heritage than by exploring its local art, music, and performances. Whether you're attending an opera, viewing classic masterpieces, or catching a live concert, here's how to experience the best of Florence's artistic scene.

📍 Uffizi Gallery

No visit to Florence is complete without exploring the **Uffizi Gallery**, home to an extraordinary collection of Renaissance art. Works by Botticelli, Michelangelo, Leonardo da Vinci, and Raphael are on display, making it one of the most visited art museums in the world. Be sure to take your time to fully appreciate the masterpieces that have shaped art history.

- 🕐 Best Time to Visit: Early morning to avoid crowds.

- 📞 +39 055 2388651

- 🖥 www.uffizi.it

- 📍 Piazzale degli Uffizi, 6, 50122 Florence.

📍 Teatro della Pergola

For those who enjoy live performances, the **Teatro della Pergola** is one of Florence's oldest and most prestigious theaters. It hosts a variety of performances, including opera, ballet, and theater, with both Italian and international productions. The theater's stunning architecture and history add an extra layer of charm to any performance.

- 🕐 Best Time to Visit: Year-round performances, check the calendar for specific events.

- 📞 +39 055 226 4313

- 🖥 www.teatrodellapergola.com

- 📍 Via della Pergola, 18, 50121 Florence.

📍 Florence Opera House (Teatro del Maggio Musicale Fiorentino)

As mentioned earlier, the **Teatro del Maggio Musicale Fiorentino** is Florence's opera house and one of Italy's most important cultural venues. It hosts a range of performances, from operas to ballet and classical music concerts. If you love music, catching a performance here is an unforgettable experience. The building itself is modern and striking, adding to the allure of any event.

- 🕐 Best Time to Visit: May, during the **Maggio Musicale Fiorentino** festival.

- 📞 +39 055 2768424

- 🖥 www.maggiofiorentino.com

- 📍 Corso Italia, 16, 50122 Florence.

📍 Florence Biennale (International Contemporary Art Exhibition)

For contemporary art lovers, the **Florence Biennale** is a must-attend event. Held every two years, it brings together international artists working in various mediums, from visual arts to digital creations. The exhibition features works from both established and emerging artists and is a great way to experience the cutting edge of the art world in the heart of Florence.

- 🕑 Best Time to Visit: Every two years, in late autumn.

- 📞 +39 055 241 968

- 🖥 www.florencebiennale.org

- 📍 Fortezza da Basso, Florence.

Florence's cultural scene is a rich tapestry of history and modernity, from its world-class museums and stunning performances to its vibrant festivals and celebrations. Whether you're catching a live performance at one of the city's historic theaters or attending a local festival, you'll find plenty of opportunities to immerse yourself in the heart of Florence's cultural life.

Chapter 9

Shopping and Souvenirs

Florence is a shopping paradise, whether you're looking for high-end fashion, unique handcrafted goods, or local treasures that tell the story of Tuscany's rich artisan history. From elegant boutiques to bustling markets, there's no shortage of shopping experiences in this beautiful city. Here's a guide to the best shopping spots and the most authentic souvenirs to bring home.

Best Shopping Spots: Malls, Markets, and Boutiques

📍 Via de' Tornabuoni

For those who love luxury shopping, **Via de' Tornabuoni** is Florence's high-end shopping street, lined with designer boutiques and upscale fashion houses. Here, you'll find world-famous brands like **Gucci**, **Prada**, **Salvatore Ferragamo**, and **Louis Vuitton**. Whether you're window shopping or splurging on a new wardrobe, this glamorous street is a must-visit for fashion enthusiasts.

- 🕐 Best Time to Visit: Early morning to avoid the crowds.

130

- 📍 Via de' Tornabuoni, Florence.

📍 The Mall Firenze

Located just outside Florence, **The Mall** is a luxury outlet mall offering steep discounts on high-end brands. If you're in the mood for designer deals, this is the place to be. With outlets for **Gucci**, **Armani**, **Fendi**, and more, you'll find upscale fashion at a fraction of the cost. The mall also has great food options, making it a convenient stop for a shopping spree outside the city center.

- 🕐 Best Time to Visit: Weekdays to avoid the weekend crowds.

- 📞 +39 055 8657775

- 🖥 www.themall.it

- 📍 Via Europa 8, 50066 Leccio Reggello, Florence.

📍 Mercato Centrale (Central Market)

If you're looking for a true Florence shopping experience, head to the **Mercato Centrale**, an iconic indoor market located near **San Lorenzo**. While it's best known for its food stalls selling fresh produce, meats, and cheeses, the market also has plenty of shops offering local products like olive oil, truffles, and artisanal pasta. Upstairs, you'll find eateries offering local delicacies, making it the perfect spot for both shopping and dining.

- 🕒 Best Time to Visit: Late morning for less crowding.

- 📞 +39 055 2399798

- 🖥 www.mercatocentrale.it

- 📍 Piazza del Mercato Centrale, 50123 Florence.

📍 San Lorenzo Market

Adjacent to the Mercato Centrale, **San Lorenzo Market** is a must-visit for anyone looking for leather goods. Florence is famous for its high-quality leather products, and at this bustling market, you'll find everything from jackets to bags and wallets, all crafted by local artisans. It's a great place to shop for a lasting souvenir that will remind you of your time in Tuscany.

- 🕒 Best Time to Visit: Early afternoon for a less crowded experience.

- 📍 Piazza San Lorenzo, Florence.

📍 **Via della Vigna Nuova and Via degli Strozzi**

For a more refined shopping experience, head to **Via della Vigna Nuova** and **Via degli Strozzi**. These elegant streets are filled with boutique stores offering high-quality fashion, jewelry, and accessories. You'll find chic shops with Italian-made goods, perfect for anyone looking to invest in something special while exploring Florence's stylish side.

- 🕐 Best Time to Visit: Late morning or early afternoon.

- 📍 Via della Vigna Nuova, Florence.

Authentic Local Crafts and One-of-a-Kind Finds

Florence is a hub of artisanal craftsmanship, and no trip to the city would be complete without picking up an authentic local craft or unique find. From handmade leather goods to beautiful jewelry and traditional ceramics, here are some of the best locally-made souvenirs to look for:

📍 **Leather Goods**

Florence is world-famous for its leather craftsmanship, and the city is brimming with shops selling high-quality leather products. At markets like **San Lorenzo Market** and boutique stores across the city, you'll find everything from jackets and handbags to wallets, belts, and gloves. The **Oltrarno** district, in particular, is home to many artisan workshops where you can watch leather artisans at work.

- 🕐 Best Time to Visit: Visit early for a quieter shopping experience.

- 📍 San Lorenzo Market and shops in Oltrarno.

📍 Florentine Paper and Stationery

Florence has a long tradition of paper-making, and you can find beautifully handcrafted stationery, journals, and paper products throughout the city. **Il Papiro**, one of the oldest paper workshops in Florence, offers stunning handcrafted paper goods made using centuries-old techniques. These are perfect gifts for those who appreciate unique, artisanal products.

- 🕐 Best Time to Visit: Midday for the full selection.

- 📞 +39 055 217870

- 🖥 www.ilpapiro.com

- 📍 Via dei Servi 30/r, Florence.

📍 Ceramics

134

Tuscan ceramics are known for their vibrant colors and traditional designs. In Florence, you'll find shops selling hand-painted ceramic plates, bowls, and decorative pieces, often featuring the iconic **Florentine yellow** and **blue** patterns. Head to **Via Santo Spirito** and **Piazza Santo Spirito**, where you'll find shops dedicated to these beautiful handmade items.

- 🕐 Best Time to Visit: Early morning to avoid crowds.

- 📍 Via Santo Spirito, Florence.

📍 Artisanal Jewelry

Florence is home to some fantastic artisan jewelers, with many independent shops offering unique, handcrafted pieces. The **Ponte Vecchio** is famous for its jewelry shops, where you'll find everything from classic gold pieces to intricate designs featuring local gemstones. For a more modern take, explore the shops around **Piazza della Signoria**, where independent designers showcase their one-of-a-kind creations.

- 🕐 Best Time to Visit: Late afternoon for fewer crowds.

- 📍 Ponte Vecchio, Florence.

📍 Tuscan Wines and Olive Oil

A great way to take home a taste of Tuscany is by purchasing local **wines** and **extra virgin olive oil**. Many stores in Florence offer bottles of local **Chianti**, **Vino Nobile di Montepulciano**, and other regional wines. You can also find top-quality **olive oils**, often paired with balsamic vinegar from **Modena**. For a truly authentic souvenir, seek out a small **vinoteca** (wine shop) where you can buy wine directly from the source.

- 🕐 Best Time to Visit: Anytime during your trip.

- 📍 Various shops throughout Florence.

Florence offers a wealth of shopping opportunities, from high-end boutiques to charming artisan markets, where you can pick up truly unique and authentic souvenirs. Whether you're hunting for handmade leather goods or local wines, these shopping spots and one-of-a-kind finds will leave you with lasting memories of your time in Tuscany.

Smart Bargaining Tips and Shopping Etiquette

Florence offers a variety of shopping experiences, from luxury boutiques to bustling markets, and while the city is known for its high-quality goods, it's always good to know a few tips to ensure you get the best deals, especially when shopping at markets or independent shops. Understanding the local shopping etiquette can also help you feel more comfortable while navigating the city's vibrant retail scene.

Smart Bargaining Tips

1. Bargaining at Markets

When shopping at open-air markets, like **San Lorenzo Market** or **Mercato di Sant'Ambrogio**, bargaining is often expected, but keep in mind that it's more of an art than a necessity. Here's how to approach bargaining in a polite and respectful way:

- **Start Low**: If you're negotiating for an item, start by offering a price lower than what you're willing to pay. This gives you room to negotiate while showing the seller that you're serious about getting a better deal.

- **Be Polite**: Always be friendly and respectful. Italians are known for their hospitality, and a smile can go a long way when bargaining.

- **Know When to Stop**: If the seller doesn't budge on the price, don't push too hard. If you're not happy with the price, it's perfectly acceptable to politely walk away. In many cases, the seller may offer a better deal as you leave.

2. Quality Over Quantity

Florence is known for its high-quality goods, especially leather, jewelry, and art. While it's tempting to find a bargain, ensure you're not compromising on quality, particularly when buying artisan or handcrafted items. Check the quality of leather goods and textiles by inspecting the stitching, feel of the material, and weight. If you're unsure about a product's authenticity, it's okay to ask for more information or for certificates of authenticity, particularly for items like high-end jewelry or art.

3. Shopping Sales and Discounts

Florence hosts seasonal sales that offer excellent discounts, typically in **January** and **July**, known as the **Saldi**. During these times, you can find up to 50-70% off on clothing, shoes, and accessories in shops across the city. If you're shopping for designer items or high-end fashion, these seasonal sales can be a great time to grab luxury pieces at lower prices.

- **Look for Red Signs**: During the sale season, shops will often display red signs announcing their sales. Be sure to check the dates and shop early to get the best selection.

- **Keep an Eye on Stock**: Some shops may display sale items separately, but others may mix sale items in with regular stock. Always ask if you're unsure whether a product is part of a discount deal.

Shopping Etiquette

1. Greeting the Shopkeeper

It's important to greet the shopkeeper when you enter a store or market stall. A simple **"Buongiorno"** (Good morning) or **"Ciao"** (Hello) is polite and appreciated. Italians take personal connections seriously, and greeting someone is a sign of respect.

- **Addressing the Seller**: Use formal titles like **Signore** (Mr.) or **Signora** (Mrs.) unless the shopkeeper initiates a more casual conversation. The use of formal language is a sign of respect and helps maintain a polite exchange.

2. Don't Expect Extended Hours

Unlike other cities, Florence has a more relaxed approach to shopping hours. Many shops, especially smaller boutiques, close for a break between **1:00 PM and 4:00 PM**, so plan your shopping accordingly. Major department stores and larger shopping centers tend to stay open longer, but always check the shop's opening hours before heading out.

- **Sunday Closures**: Most shops are closed on Sundays, except in the more touristy areas. If you're planning to shop on a Sunday, head to the city center or major shopping streets, where stores are likely to remain open.

3. Paying for Your Purchases

Cash is still widely accepted in Florence, but credit cards are commonly used for larger purchases. Some small shops or markets might only accept cash, so it's a good idea to carry a small amount of cash on hand for quick purchases.

- **Tipping**: Tipping is not mandatory, but rounding up your bill or leaving a small tip (1-2 euros) for good service is appreciated, particularly in restaurants and cafes.

4. Be Aware of Fake Goods

Florence is a city filled with artisan-made leather goods, fashion, and art. However, it's also important to be cautious of counterfeit products, especially in high-traffic tourist areas. Ensure that you're purchasing authentic items by shopping at reputable stores or market stalls known for selling quality goods.

- **Ask Questions**: When in doubt, don't hesitate to ask the seller about the authenticity of the item, especially if it seems too cheap for a high-quality product. A genuine leather jacket, for example, should feel substantial and have a particular scent that distinguishes it from synthetic alternatives.

Shopping in Florence can be a rewarding and enjoyable experience, especially if you understand the local shopping customs and know when to bargain and when to pay the asking price. By respecting the city's etiquette and being mindful of the quality and authenticity of what you're buying, you'll leave Florence with some beautiful and meaningful souvenirs.

Chapter 10

Travel with a Conscience: Sustainable Tourism

Florence, with its stunning beauty and rich history, is a destination that draws millions of travelers each year. However, as tourism grows, it's crucial to embrace sustainable travel practices to preserve the city's cultural heritage and natural environment for future generations. Here's how you can enjoy all that Florence has to offer while minimizing your environmental impact and supporting the local community.

Eco-Friendly Activities and Green Travel Options

Florence offers a variety of eco-friendly activities that allow you to explore the city's history and natural beauty while keeping sustainability in mind.

1. Walking Tours

Florence is a compact and walkable city, making it the perfect place to explore on foot. Walking tours not only allow you to take in the beauty of Florence at your own pace but also reduce your carbon footprint. Join a **guided walking tour** to learn about the city's history and culture, or simply

142

take a self-guided stroll through the **historic center** to see landmarks like the **Duomo**, **Ponte Vecchio**, and **Palazzo Pitti**.

- 🕒 Best Time to Visit: Early morning or late afternoon to avoid crowds and enjoy the peace of the city.

2. Cycling Tours and Bike Rentals
Cycling is an environmentally friendly way to explore Florence's streets and the surrounding Tuscan countryside. There are many bike tours available that allow you to see the city's top attractions or venture further into the hills of **Chianti** and **Fiesole**. Rent a bike and navigate Florence's bike lanes or enjoy a scenic ride through the beautiful landscapes of Tuscany.

- 🕒 Best Time to Visit: Spring and fall, when the weather is mild and perfect for cycling.

3. Eco-Friendly Museums and Experiences
Many museums and cultural experiences in Florence are dedicated to promoting sustainability. For example, **Museo Leonardo da Vinci** showcases innovative ways of thinking about technology and sustainability, while the **Florence Botanical Garden** teaches about the importance of plant

143

conservation. Support these cultural institutions that strive to raise awareness about ecological issues.

- ⏲ Best Time to Visit: Weekdays for a more relaxed visit.

4. Green Tours of Florence

Several companies now offer "green" tours in Florence, focusing on sustainable travel practices. These tours prioritize local and eco-friendly transportation, such as electric vehicles and bicycles, and often include visits to organic farms, vineyards, or sustainable artisans' workshops where you can learn about eco-conscious production processes.

Supporting Local Businesses and Communities

One of the most rewarding aspects of sustainable tourism is the opportunity to support local businesses and communities. Here's how you can make a positive impact while enjoying Florence:

1. Shop at Local Markets

Florence is home to bustling local markets, such as **Mercato Centrale** and **Piazza San Lorenzo Market**, where you can

144

find fresh produce, local foods, and handcrafted goods. By shopping at these markets, you help support local farmers, artisans, and food producers while reducing your reliance on mass-produced goods. Look for handmade leather products, organic olive oils, or fresh produce grown in the region.

- 🕐 Best Time to Visit: Early mornings for the best selection.

2. Dining at Local Restaurants and Cafes

Choose to dine at local, family-owned restaurants and cafes that focus on sustainable sourcing and organic ingredients. Many eateries in Florence embrace farm-to-table dining, offering seasonal dishes made with locally sourced ingredients. By supporting these businesses, you contribute to the local economy while enjoying authentic Tuscan cuisine.

- 🕐 Best Time to Visit: Dinner for a relaxed, authentic experience in the evening.

3. Participate in Artisan Workshops

Florence is known for its craftsmanship, particularly in leather, ceramics, and jewelry. Consider taking a **workshop** or **tour** to learn about these local crafts and purchase handmade goods directly from artisans. This supports small businesses and ensures the preservation of traditional Italian craftsmanship.

- 🕐 Best Time to Visit: Year-round, especially for interactive experiences.

How to Minimize Your Carbon Footprint While Traveling

As travelers, we have a responsibility to reduce our environmental impact and minimize our carbon footprint. Here are a few tips on how to be more eco-conscious while traveling in Florence:

1. Use Public Transportation

While Florence is a walkable city, public transportation can be a great way to travel longer distances sustainably. The city has an efficient **bus** and **tram** system, and using these modes of transport can reduce the number of cars on the road. If you're venturing into the Tuscan countryside, consider taking a **train** to nearby towns like **Fiesole** or **Siena**.

- 🕐 Best Time to Visit: Off-peak times to avoid overcrowding and make the most of the eco-friendly transport options.

2. Stay in Eco-Friendly Accommodations

Florence offers a growing number of **eco-friendly hotels** and accommodations that focus on sustainability, including energy-efficient buildings, waste reduction, and water conservation. Look for **green certifications** or **eco-lodges** that have a commitment to minimizing their environmental impact.

- ⏲ Best Time to Visit: Anytime, but be sure to check sustainability ratings when booking.

3. Reduce Plastic Waste

Carry a **reusable water bottle** to minimize plastic waste, and be mindful of single-use plastics when dining out or shopping. Florence has many refill stations for water, and many cafes offer discounts for customers who bring their own reusable cups.

- ⏲ Best Time to Visit: Always—be mindful of your environmental footprint throughout your stay.

Tips for Responsible Tourism

As a responsible tourist, it's important to not only reduce your environmental impact but also respect the local culture and heritage. Here are some tips to make your visit to Florence more ethical and respectful:

1. Respect Local Culture and Traditions

Take the time to learn about the customs, traditions, and etiquette of Florence. Be mindful of dress codes, especially when visiting churches or religious sites. Modesty is appreciated, so ensure that shoulders and knees are covered when entering places of worship.

2. Support Ethical Businesses

Look for businesses that prioritize ethical practices, such as fair wages, sustainable sourcing, and community investment. Many Florence-based shops, restaurants, and tours offer sustainable or ethical products and services, and choosing to support these businesses helps promote positive change.

3. Be Mindful of Waste and Recycling

Florence has a robust recycling system, and it's important to dispose of your waste properly. Look for the **color-coded bins** throughout the city—separate your plastic, paper, and organic waste. Practicing responsible waste disposal not only helps keep the city clean but also reduces its environmental impact.

Traveling with a conscience in Florence means not only enjoying the beauty of the city but also doing your part to preserve it. By choosing eco-friendly activities, supporting local businesses, and reducing your carbon footprint, you can ensure that Florence remains a vibrant and sustainable destination for future generations.

Chapter 11

Practical Information and Travel Essentials

When traveling to Florence, it's essential to know the practical details that can help make your trip smoother and more enjoyable. From managing your money to staying connected, this chapter provides the key information you need for a hassle-free experience.

Currency, and Money-Saving Tips

Currency

Florence, like the rest of Italy, uses the **Euro (€)** as its official currency. Most places in Florence accept credit and debit cards, but it's always a good idea to have some cash on hand, especially when visiting markets, small shops, or local restaurants.

- **ATMs**: You'll find plenty of **ATMs** (Bancomat) around the city, typically offering competitive exchange rates. Always check for any fees your bank might charge for international withdrawals.

- **Exchanging Money**: If you need to exchange cash, avoid exchanging at airports or exchange bureaus in tourist-heavy areas, as the rates tend to be less favorable. Instead, look for exchange offices located outside major tourist centers or use a **foreign currency card** to withdraw money at a better rate.

Money-Saving Tips

Florence can be an expensive destination, but there are plenty of ways to save money while experiencing all the beauty it has to offer:

- **Free Attractions**: Many museums and landmarks, such as the **Florence Cathedral** and **Piazza del Duomo**, are free to visit. Additionally, Florence's vibrant **markets** offer a fun, no-cost experience.

- **City Passes**: Consider purchasing a **Firenze Card**, which offers skip-the-line access to many of Florence's top attractions, including the **Uffizi Gallery**, **Palazzo Pitti**, and more. It also offers access to public transport, saving you time and money.

- **Eat Like a Local**: Avoid tourist traps near major landmarks and head to local trattorias, pizzerias, and markets for affordable yet delicious meals.

Emergency Numbers, Safety Advice, and Local Laws

Emergency Numbers

It's always important to know the emergency contact numbers in case of an emergency while traveling:

- **Police**: 112 (EU emergency number)

- **Ambulance**: 118

- **Fire Department**: 115

- **General Emergency Services**: 112

Safety Advice

Florence is generally a safe city, but like any popular tourist destination, it's important to stay vigilant:

- **Pickpockets**: Keep an eye on your belongings, especially in crowded areas like **Piazza del Duomo**, **Ponte Vecchio**, and on public transport. Use a money belt or keep valuables in a secure, front-pocket location.

- **Avoid Dark Alleys**: Stick to well-lit streets at night, particularly if you're unfamiliar with the area. The city is safe, but it's always best to be cautious, especially when exploring after dark.

Local Laws and Customs

To make your stay in Florence as smooth as possible, here are some local laws and customs to be aware of:

- **Drinking in Public**: Drinking alcohol in public places like streets, parks, and squares is generally prohibited in Florence, except during designated times or events. Always drink at licensed establishments like bars or restaurants.

- **Smoking**: Smoking is prohibited indoors in public spaces, including restaurants, cafes, and public transport. Look for designated smoking areas.

- **Dress Codes**: When visiting religious sites, be respectful of local traditions by covering shoulders and knees. This is especially important at places like **Santa Maria del Fiore (The Duomo)** and **Basilica di Santa Croce**.

Internet Access, and Charging Devices

Internet Access

Staying connected in Florence is relatively easy, with many cafes, restaurants, and public spaces offering **free Wi-Fi**. However, some places might ask you to make a purchase before giving you access. Here's how to stay connected:

- **Public Wi-Fi**: Free Wi-Fi is available in various public spaces, including **Piazza della Repubblica**, **Piazza San Lorenzo**, and many coffee shops.

- **SIM Cards**: If you need mobile data, buying a local **SIM card** is an affordable option. Major providers like **TIM**, **Vodafone**, and **Wind** offer prepaid plans for tourists. You can purchase a SIM card at the airport or at mobile phone shops around the city.

- **Portable Wi-Fi**: For ease, consider renting a portable Wi-Fi device, especially if you plan to visit the Tuscan countryside or need to stay connected while traveling outside of Florence.

Charging Devices

When traveling, it's important to ensure your devices stay charged. Here's what you need to know:

- **Power Plugs**: Italy uses **Type C, F, and L** plugs, with a voltage of 230V and a frequency of 50Hz.

Make sure to bring a universal plug adapter to charge your devices.

- **Charging Stations**: Many cafes and public spaces in Florence have **charging stations** for devices, but it's always a good idea to bring your own portable charger in case you need it.

- **Charging Fees**: Some cafes or restaurants may charge a small fee for device charging, so be sure to ask first if you're not sure.

Packing Guide Based on Florence's Climate

Florence experiences a Mediterranean climate, with hot, dry summers and mild winters. Here's a packing guide to help you prepare for the weather and make the most of your time in the city.

Spring (March to May)

Spring in Florence is mild, with average temperatures ranging from **10°C (50°F)** to **20°C (68°F)**. It's a great time to visit as the city is less crowded.

- **What to Pack**: Light layers, a jacket for cooler evenings, comfortable walking shoes, and an umbrella in case of rain.

- **Pro Tip**: Bring a scarf for cooler mornings and evenings.

Summer (June to August)

Florence can get quite hot in summer, with temperatures soaring up to **35°C (95°F)** or more. Expect lots of sunshine and high tourist traffic during these months.

- **What to Pack**: Lightweight, breathable clothing, sunscreen, sunglasses, a hat, and comfortable walking shoes for sightseeing.

- **Pro Tip**: Bring a reusable water bottle to stay hydrated and seek shade during the hottest parts of the day (usually between 1 PM and 4 PM).

Fall (September to November)

Fall in Florence is mild and pleasant, with temperatures ranging from **15°C (59°F)** to **25°C (77°F)**. It's a wonderful time to visit as the summer crowds begin to thin out.

- **What to Pack**: Light layers, a jacket for evening walks, comfortable shoes for walking, and a scarf for the cooler evenings.

- **Pro Tip**: The fall is harvest time, so bring a camera to capture the stunning colors of the vineyards and hills.

Winter (December to February)

Winter in Florence is cool but rarely freezing, with temperatures ranging from **3°C (37°F)** to **12°C (54°F)**. Expect fewer tourists during this time, making it an ideal time for a quieter visit.

- **What to Pack**: Warm layers, a heavier jacket, gloves, and a scarf. It can get chilly in the evenings, so don't forget a coat.

- **Pro Tip**: Although it doesn't snow often, be prepared for occasional rain, so pack an umbrella.

By being prepared with the right practical information and packing essentials, you can make the most of your trip to Florence while ensuring your safety, comfort, and convenience throughout your stay.

Chapter 12

Itineraries and Day Trips

Florence is an incredibly versatile destination, offering endless opportunities to explore the city itself and the stunning landscapes of Tuscany. Whether you have a long weekend or a full week, this chapter will guide you through the best itineraries to make the most of your time in and around Florence. You'll also find day trips and excursions to nearby towns and hidden gems, as well as seasonal recommendations for when to visit for the best local experiences.

Perfect 3-Day, 5-Day, and Week-Long Plans

3-Day Florence Itinerary

A 3-day trip to Florence will give you enough time to dive into the city's rich culture and history, while still leaving you with the opportunity to experience its charming neighborhoods and vibrant atmosphere.

Day 1: Explore the Historic Center

- **Morning**: Start your day with a visit to the **Duomo** and climb to the top of the **Campanile** for stunning views of Florence. Afterward, head to the **Baptistery of St. John** to admire its intricate mosaics.

- **Afternoon**: Visit the **Uffizi Gallery**, one of the world's most famous art museums, to see masterpieces by Botticelli, Leonardo da Vinci, and Michelangelo.

- **Evening**: Take a leisurely walk across the **Ponte Vecchio**, the historic bridge lined with jewelry shops, and enjoy dinner at a local trattoria in the **Oltrarno** district.

Day 2: Art, Gardens, and Views

- **Morning**: Visit the **Accademia Gallery** to see Michelangelo's iconic *David*. Afterward, head to the **San Lorenzo Market** for a taste of local food and shopping.

- **Afternoon**: Spend a couple of hours at the **Boboli Gardens**, enjoying the peaceful atmosphere and panoramic views of the city.

- **Evening**: Walk up to **Piazzale Michelangelo** for sunset, offering the most breathtaking view of Florence. Dinner in the **Piazza della Signoria** area.

Day 3: Off-the-Beaten-Path and Local Markets

- **Morning**: Visit the **Basilica di Santa Croce**, the final resting place of famous Florentines like Galileo and Michelangelo.

- **Afternoon**: Explore the **Mercato Centrale** for lunch, offering local delicacies like fresh pasta, porchetta sandwiches, and regional cheeses.

- **Evening**: End your trip with a visit to the **Pitti Palace** and **Palazzina della Meridiana**. If you have time, enjoy a night out in the **Santa Maria Novella** district, where you'll find great bars and cafes.

5-Day Florence Itinerary

With five days, you can go deeper into Florence's cultural landmarks and still have time for a relaxing day trip to the Tuscan countryside.

Day 1: Classic Florence

Follow the same plan as **Day 1** in the 3-Day Itinerary: Start with the **Duomo** and explore the **Uffizi Gallery** in the morning. Spend the evening walking across the **Ponte Vecchio**.

Day 2: Museums and Views

159

Spend the morning at the **Accademia Gallery** and then take a stroll through the **Boboli Gardens** in the afternoon. Enjoy a sunset at **Piazzale Michelangelo**.

Day 3: Tuscan Food and Local Life

- **Morning**: Begin with a visit to the **Mercato Centrale**, and enjoy a guided food tour through the market to sample fresh produce, local cheeses, and Tuscan olive oils.

- **Afternoon**: After lunch, take a leisurely walk around **Santa Croce** and explore the surrounding artisan shops.

- **Evening**: Enjoy dinner at a local **farm-to-table** restaurant for an authentic experience of Tuscan flavors.

Day 4: Day Trip to Fiesole

Take a short trip to **Fiesole**, a hilltop town just outside Florence. Explore the **Roman Theater**, visit the **Archaeological Museum**, and hike up to the **Fiesole Hill** for spectacular views of Florence.

- **Evening**: Return to Florence and have dinner at a restaurant in the **Piazza Santo Spirito** area, known for its relaxed vibe.

Day 5: Hidden Gems and Relaxation

- **Morning**: Spend your last day exploring the **Oltrarno** district, visiting lesser-known spots like the **Stibbert Museum** or browsing artisan workshops.

- **Afternoon**: Take a leisurely afternoon walk along the **Arno River** or visit the **Bardini Gardens** for beautiful views of Florence.

- **Evening**: End your trip with a dinner at a traditional **Osteria**, savoring a final meal of *Bistecca alla Fiorentina* and Tuscan wine.

Week-Long Florence Itinerary

A full week in Florence offers the opportunity to experience the city's iconic attractions and nearby towns at a more leisurely pace.

Days 1-3: Follow the same plan as the **3-Day Itinerary** for your first three days in Florence. You'll hit the key spots, including the **Uffizi Gallery**, **Duomo**, **Ponte Vecchio**, and

Boboli Gardens, while soaking up the atmosphere of the city.

Day 4: Day Trip to the Chianti Region
Take a scenic drive to the **Chianti region** and visit some of Tuscany's most renowned vineyards. Take a wine tour and enjoy a Tuscan wine-tasting session paired with local cheeses and meats.

- **Afternoon**: Visit charming towns like **Greve in Chianti** or **Radda in Chianti**, known for their picturesque streets and medieval charm.

- **Evening**: Return to Florence and enjoy a quiet dinner at a trattoria in the **San Frediano** neighborhood.

Day 5: Day Trip to Pisa or Siena

- **Morning**: Head to **Pisa** to see the famous **Leaning Tower** and **Piazza dei Miracoli**.

- **Afternoon**: Alternatively, take a trip to **Siena**, one of Tuscany's most beautiful medieval cities. Visit the **Piazza del Campo** and **Siena Cathedral**, and explore its winding streets.

- **Evening**: Return to Florence for dinner at a local bistro.

Day 6: Visit Lucca and the Tuscan Countryside
Spend the day exploring the charming city of **Lucca**, surrounded by well-preserved Renaissance walls. Rent a bike and cycle along the city's famous ramparts, visit **Torre Guinigi** for panoramic views, and stroll through the **Piazza dell'Anfiteatro**.

- **Evening**: Return to Florence and dine in the **Piazza della Signoria** area, soaking in the evening ambiance.

Day 7: Relax and Discover Hidden Gems
On your last day in Florence, take it easy and explore the quieter, lesser-known parts of the city. Walk around the **Boboli Gardens**, visit the **Bargello Museum**, and wander through the artisan shops in the **Oltrarno** district.

- **Evening**: End your week with a sunset at **Piazzale Michelangelo**, followed by a leisurely dinner at a traditional Florentine restaurant.

Suggested Day Trips and Excursions Nearby

1. Fiesole

A short bus or taxi ride from Florence, **Fiesole** is a hilltop town with fantastic views of the city. Visit the **Roman**

Theater, enjoy the scenic walks, and explore the **Archaeological Museum**.

2. Siena

A UNESCO World Heritage site, **Siena** is famous for its medieval architecture and the historic **Piazza del Campo**, where the **Palio horse race** is held twice a year. Don't miss the stunning **Siena Cathedral** and the **Torre del Mangia**.

3. Pisa

Home to the world-famous **Leaning Tower**, **Pisa** is a must-see for anyone visiting Tuscany. Explore the **Piazza dei Miracoli** and visit the **Baptistery** and **Camposanto Monumentale**.

4. Chianti Region

For wine lovers, a day trip to the **Chianti wine region** is perfect. Take a vineyard tour, enjoy wine tastings, and explore the charming towns of **Greve** and **Radda**.

5. Lucca

A charming medieval town, **Lucca** offers great shopping, beautiful parks, and the famous **city walls** where you can rent a bike and cycle around the city.

Seasonal Travel Plans with Local Insights

Spring (March - May):

Spring is one of the best times to visit Florence. The weather is mild, and the city is not yet overcrowded with tourists. Visit **Boboli Gardens** and enjoy the flowers in bloom.

Summer (June - August):

Florence can be hot and crowded in summer, but it's also when many of the festivals and outdoor events take place. Enjoy summer evenings at open-air concerts and festivals like **Maggio Musicale Fiorentino**.

Fall (September - November):

The fall months are ideal for exploring the Tuscan countryside, with the vineyards turning vibrant shades of red and gold. Enjoy a wine-tasting tour and the harvest season.

Winter (December - February):

While winter can be cold, it's also when Florence is less crowded. Enjoy Christmas markets, seasonal events, and fewer tourists at museums and galleries.

These itineraries and day trips provide the perfect balance of exploring Florence's cultural gems and venturing out to discover the beauty of Tuscany. Whether you're in town for a few days or a week, there's something for everyone to enjoy.

Chapter 13

Insider Tips and Tricks

Florence is a city brimming with charm, history, and beauty, but like any popular tourist destination, it can also have its fair share of tourist traps. To truly experience the best the city has to offer without falling into the common pitfalls, here are some insider tips and tricks that will make your trip feel more authentic, local, and cost-effective.

Avoiding Tourist Traps

1. Steer Clear of Overpriced Restaurants Near Major Attractions

While it's tempting to sit at a cafe with a view of the **Piazza del Duomo** or **Ponte Vecchio**, be aware that restaurants in these areas often charge premium prices for subpar food. Instead, explore the charming side streets in neighborhoods like **Oltrarno** or **San Niccolò**, where you'll find authentic and reasonably priced eateries. The quality of the food is just as good, if not better, and you'll avoid the hefty tourist markup.

2. Skip the Lines with Smart Timing

Some of Florence's most famous attractions, like the **Uffizi Gallery** and **Accademia Gallery**, can have long lines, especially during peak tourist seasons. To avoid waiting in line, try visiting these spots early in the morning or later in the afternoon when crowds tend to thin out. Another great tip is to book tickets online in advance, which not only guarantees your entry but also allows you to skip the line altogether.

3. Beware of Tourist Shops Selling "Authentic" Souvenirs

Many shops near major attractions sell mass-produced items marketed as "authentic." If you're looking for genuine Florentine craftsmanship, skip the souvenir shops and head to areas like **San Lorenzo Market** or the **Oltrarno district**, where you can find locally made leather goods, ceramics, and art. Shopping directly from artisans ensures that you're purchasing high-quality, handmade products.

4. Don't Buy Bottled Water at Tourist Sites

Bottled water is often overpriced at tourist-heavy areas, so instead of grabbing a bottle near popular attractions, look for public water fountains (known as **nasoni**) located throughout the city. Florence has numerous drinking fountains with clean, fresh water that's completely free! Carry a reusable water bottle and refill it whenever you need.

How to Blend In Like a Local

1. Dress Smart and Avoid the "Tourist Look"

Florence is a city where style matters. While you don't need to be overly formal, locals tend to dress neatly, even for casual outings. Avoid wearing athletic gear or overly casual clothes like flip-flops or sweatpants, especially if you're dining out or visiting more upscale venues. Instead, opt for comfortable yet stylish outfits, and wear comfortable shoes for all the walking you'll do in the city.

2. Master the Art of the Italian Coffee Break

When you stop for coffee in Florence, don't order a cappuccino after breakfast. Italians typically drink cappuccino in the morning, and ordering one in the afternoon or evening will mark you as a tourist. If you want coffee later in the day, stick with an espresso, which is the more traditional choice. Also, when ordering coffee, expect to stand at the bar, especially in smaller cafes. It's common to pay first, then drink your coffee standing at the counter.

3. Know Your Meal Times

Florence follows a typical Italian eating schedule: **lunch** is from 1:00 PM to 3:00 PM, and **dinner** is usually served between 7:30 PM and 9:00 PM. If you're looking for a meal outside of these hours, you might find that many restaurants are closed or offer limited menus. Try to stick to these times to avoid feeling rushed or limited in your dining options.

4. Speak a Few Words in Italian

While many people in Florence speak English, making an effort to use basic Italian phrases will endear you to the locals. Simple greetings like **"Buongiorno"** (Good morning) and **"Grazie"** (Thank you) go a long way. If you're unsure, a friendly **"Parli inglese?"** (Do you speak English?) can help you get started.

Saving Money Without Sacrificing Experience

1. Take Advantage of Free Attractions

Florence is home to many free attractions that allow you to experience the city's culture without spending a dime. Take a walk through **Piazza del Duomo**, enjoy the stunning **Piazza della Signoria**, or visit **Piazzale Michelangelo** for panoramic views of the city. Additionally, you can enjoy **churches** like **Santa Croce** or **Santa Maria Novella**, which often have free entry (though a small donation is appreciated).

2. Use the Firenze Card Wisely

If you're planning to visit several museums and galleries in Florence, consider purchasing the **Firenze Card**, which offers skip-the-line access and entry to over 70 museums and cultural attractions. It can save you time and money, especially if you plan to explore Florence's top sights in a few days. Just be sure to plan your visits carefully to make the most out of the card's 72-hour validity period.

3. Eat Well on a Budget

Florence is known for its rich culinary traditions, and there's no need to break the bank to enjoy delicious food. Instead of dining in tourist areas, head to local spots that serve traditional, affordable Tuscan dishes. **Osteria Santo Spirito** and **Trattoria 4 Leoni** are great options for experiencing authentic Florentine cuisine at reasonable prices. For an even cheaper option, grab a tasty **panino** (sandwich) at **All'Antico Vinaio** or visit the **Mercato Centrale** for a variety of affordable food stalls.

4. Explore the City by Foot or Public Transport

Florence is best explored on foot, and walking is free! Most of the city's top attractions, such as the **Duomo**, **Uffizi Gallery**, and **Ponte Vecchio**, are within walking distance of each other. If you do need to travel further, use the **Florence bus system**, which is both affordable and efficient. A **single ride** costs around €1.50, making it a cost-effective alternative to taxis.

5. Avoid Tourist Shops for Souvenirs

If you want to bring home a souvenir, skip the touristy shops near major attractions, where prices tend to be inflated. Instead, explore the artisan shops in the **Oltrarno** district, where you'll find high-quality leather goods, jewelry, and ceramics. These handmade items are often more affordable and much more authentic than mass-produced trinkets sold in crowded tourist areas.

By following these insider tips and tricks, you'll be able to experience Florence like a local—avoiding tourist traps, blending in seamlessly with the city's culture, and saving money without sacrificing the essence of your trip. Florence's charm lies in its authenticity, and with a little local knowledge, you can make the most of your time in this beautiful city.

Conclusion

Florence offers much more than just a destination—it is an experience that stays with you. From its awe-inspiring art and timeless architecture to the charming, narrow streets filled with centuries of history, this city creates a lasting impression long after you've left.

By using the insights and tips from this guide, you've been able to uncover Florence's best-kept secrets, avoid the usual tourist traps, and immerse yourself in the authentic experiences the city has to offer. Whether you stood in awe before Michelangelo's *David*, wandered through the tranquil Boboli Gardens, or shared a delicious meal with locals, Florence has provided you with memories that will last a lifetime.

Florence is a city that invites discovery again and again. No matter how many times you visit, there's always something new waiting to be explored—be it a hidden café, a quaint neighborhood, or an unexpected local event. It's a place that continues to unfold its stories, and you've only just begun to scratch the surface.

When you look back on your time in Florence, let the small yet beautiful moments stand out: the aroma of freshly baked bread, the laughter shared over a glass of wine, or the golden glow of the city as the sun sets. These moments make Florence a city like no other.

Thank you for using this guide to navigate your way through Florence. I hope your journey was as magical as it was memorable, and that you leave with not just souvenirs, but a piece of Florence in your heart. Safe travels, and may the beauty of this city always inspire you.

Printed in Dunstable, United Kingdom